PLAYWRITING

A  DRAMA RESOURCE
HOW-TO BOOK

PLAYWRITING

A Study in
Choices and Challenges

by

Paul McCusker

Author of *Catacombs, Snapshots and Portraits,*
Family Outings, A Work in Progress, and more.

KANSAS CITY, MO 64141

10 9 8 7 6 5 4 3 2 1

Contents

Introduction

OK, so you want to write plays. Maybe plays for your church, your local theatre group, perhaps for any group anywhere that has a need for a play with a distinctive *moral* perspective: a worldview born out of Holy Scripture, the great creeds, the writings of those spiritual fathers who came before you, or your own personal experience with Jesus Christ. You want to write plays to fulfill that persistent itch that won't be scratched until you put pen to paper, or keyboard to computer. You want to write plays because a deep stirring—a *calling*—demands that you write them.

Or you want to write plays because the committee took a vote and decided that, since you wrote that heart-wrenching poem for the Mother's Day banquet, which makes you the closest thing to a writer they know, *you* should write the play for the upcoming Summer Arts program.

Maybe you want to write plays because . . . well, you want to write plays.

But there's a nagging feeling that you can't do it unless you learn all the "secrets" of playwriting—or read the *Ten Steps to an Award-Winning Play*—or reread that article called "Paint-by-Number Plots and Characterizations"—and then you'll have guaranteed results, right?

No, not exactly.

The good news about how-to books like this one is that they can point you in many of the right directions for writing the play you want to write (or at least help you understand why you're *not* writing the play you want). The bad news about how-to books like this one is that they can't crawl into your skin, assess your talent, abilities, dreams, desires, passions, and experiences to guarantee that what you write will hit its mark each and every time.

But that doesn't mean we can't explore some basic truths about playwriting together and come up with ways to be better writers.

Perceptively and Knowledgeably

Without anyone saying so, you know that writing can be an insecure activity. While you're hoping to write something that will change civilization as we know it, the trash needs to be taken out, the furniture needs to be dusted, the lawn needs to be mowed, and your family thinks you've lost your mind for spending so much time on something that may never earn you a single penny. OK, maybe changing civilization as we know it isn't an attainable goal. But there are other goals to consider. Like writing *perceptively* and *knowledgeably*.

More than a couple of goals, being perceptive and knowledgeable are elements of *being* a writer at all. You must be perceptive in your understanding of humanity and be knowledgeable about your characters and the situations you've dropped them into. And the audience must sense your perceptiveness and knowledgeability, or why should they care about your work?

Writing perceptively and knowledgeably help make plays successful. At least, it's true in what we call the secular market. It should be truer in the Christian market. Writers with a Christian viewpoint are in touch with the very Creator and through Him and His Word should have *more* insight into the human condition than those who never had that resource.

My father-in-law, a man who is more interested in mathematics and the barometric pressure than the arts, casually observed that "entertainment needs to give us *insight* into our lives or make us *forget* about our lives altogether."

That gentleman knows a lot more about plays than a lot of playwrights.

To write a play that is both perceptive and knowledgeable will fulfill your desire as a playwright and the audience's desire as an audience.

Yet those two words shouldn't be used lightly. Years of study and writing, thousands of abandoned words and ideas may be what it takes to reach that point when what you've written may mysteriously but wonderfully connect with your audience.

But Why a Play, of All Things?

You could write a poem, a short story, a novel, a screenplay—so why drama for the stage? It's a question worth answering before you continue.

Not all ideas are suited for the stage. A novel is very *internal* in its ability to jump in and out of the minds of its characters. The story can leap miles, even light-years, to another location in just a word, a sentence, or a chapter. Movies can do the same thing with only a blink of the camera's eye. Fast cuts, fast scenes, all displaying a visual plethora of ideas and emotions—often without a single word being said.

So, why a play?

Because a play communicates human insight and truth in ways other forms of communication can't. Plays have an *immediacy*—as living, breathing actors (your characters) draw the audience into their emotions and actions onstage. It is reality in front of your audience's eyes: demanding them to be attentive with all of their senses as time progresses from a remarkably engaging present into an unknown future.

In his book *Producing and Directing Drama for the Church*, Rob Rucker aligns the immediacy of drama with the methodology that Jesus himself used: "storytelling, object lessons, and audience involvement."[1] Jesus drew His audience in by playing out a living drama—a drama He himself created perceptively and knowledgeably.

Funny how that works.

Learning as We Go

Each and every play offers its own challenges with its plot turns or characters or dialogue. Anyone who has ever seen his or her own play performed has probably walked away wondering, "How in the world did I ever go so far astray from what I intended to do?" Or "What was I thinking when I let my character say *that?*" Or "Where were my best sensibilities when I thought the audience would accept such a *lame* turning point in the plot?"

If you persist in writing for the stage, you'll find that some of your work is good and some is downright mediocre. Hopefully, though, you'll learn how to tell the difference between the two. And in learning, you'll understand the *choices* you made in your writing that caused your work to be one or the other.

That's what writing's all about, isn't it? Choices. Unique choices that vary from person to person, project to project. And writing a play is a series of very individual choices you make as you answer a series of specific questions. With those answers come new questions—and challenges—as you have to think through new answers until you have reached your goal. Does he tell her *now* that he's an alcoholic, or is there a better place to drop in that bit of information for greater impact? Should he be an alcoholic at all, or is that too predictable? Maybe he should be a spy. No, wait a minute, this is a play about a family coming to grips with change—why would I put a spy in it? He's not a spy; he's a mail carrier. Yes . . . a mail carrier who compulsively reads other people's mail. And . . . and one day he discovers that his wife is in love with a store clerk in another zip code. So he . . .

So he *what?*

Choices.

The goal for this book is to help you make some of the *right* choices, perceptively and knowledgeably.

How Will We Do That?

In the pages to come we'll talk about the fundamentals of play-writing, characters and dialogue. We'll consider ideas and stories. We'll look at the *act* of writing: its promises and pitfalls. Along the way, we'll examine the spiritual ramifications, with an eye to writing in the context of our churches. And there'll be some exercises for you to try, just for practice. There are even some clever quotes from writers you've never heard of, so you'll think I'm extremely intelligent and well-read.

But most of all we'll be dealing with choices.

So your *first* choice is whether or not to come along.

ONE

Foundations

It may well be that the author who claims to write neither for patron nor public but for himself has done our art incalculable harm and bred up infinite charlatans by teaching us to emphasize the public's duty of "recognition" instead of the artist's duty to teach and delight.

—C. S. Lewis[2]

Many writers live a schizophrenic existence—two equal halves in the same person. Half is a *pretentious artiste* who wants nothing more than to be recognized for innovative playwriting. The other half is a mercenary hack-writer who merely wants to get the job done, get paid, and go home. The first half has lofty ideas of changing theatre as we know it forever by being true to his or her artistic *vision*. The second half is a stubborn craftsman who could care less about the *vision* if it gets in the way of the dramatic *drive* of the story. These two characters are constantly at war with each other.

There has always been tension between *art* and *craft*. Why? Because one engages a seemingly unlimited imaginative experience while the other wishes to constrain that experience within the confines of structure and form.

There's nothing new in that tension.

It could be said that God had an artistic vision of creation, but it was His craftsmanship that brought it about.

Art vs. Craft

Playwright Nigel Forde addressed this conflict well when he noted that art and craft have been disputed "almost as often as the line dividing verse and prose. Craft knows exactly what its end is, and can be judged successful or otherwise by how well it has achieved its end. Its techniques and its results are analyzable in objective terms . . . What two people get from a performance of *All's Well That Ends Well* is likely to be far more differentiated than what the same two people get from looking at the most expensive of kitchen units."[3]

It can be likened to a dresser. You may buy one that is well-built—the drawers open and close, the bottoms don't fall out when you put your clothes in them, and it doesn't collapse under the weight of whatever you may put on the top. In terms of functional craftsmanship, it does its job. But the *artistry* of that functional dresser compared to an ornate, intricately designed William & Mary Oak Chest created in the 17th century may cause some debate.

"Art requires attention," Forde goes on to write, "a hearing, if it is allowed to work on us as it should: it cannot be used. Oscar Wilde remarked that all art is useless. By that he did not mean 'no good' as we might mean today, but rather that it was revelatory as opposed to functional. Its effect was not measurable. Outside a farm in the village where I grew up was the rotting hulk of a truck that had been there for perhaps ten years. It was 'useless' to the farmer, but it was paradise to us."[4]

An Unsettling Idea

Forde's concept may be unsettling for many Christians because it's too subjective and slippery for their tastes; particularly for those who view drama as a measurable means to an end. In other words, they think it's worthwhile only as long as a certain number of people come to the altar to accept Jesus at the end of the play.

You know how it is: there are Christians who want plays that *literally* show all the Christians as good guys and non-Christians (from the "world") as bad guys. They want plays that will directly proclaim the name of Jesus on every page and be certain that the steps to salvation are explained clearly by one of the good guys (resulting in, of course, the bad guys falling to their knees to receive the offer of boundless grace . . . as one hopes the audience will).

You've seen plays like that. Maybe you've already written one or two of them. I have.

It's easy to understand the desire of church leaders and members to use drama this way, and one cannot fault their good intentions to bring people to Christ. Unfortunately, those good intentions tend to rely on the *power* of drama without an understanding of what makes drama powerful in the first place. It isn't a character doing a monologue containing the "Four Spiritual Laws." Nor is it that "moment of truth" when one character shares John 3:16 with another. (Any preacher can do that from the pulpit on Sunday morning. Why not save your money on costumes and sets?) The *power* of drama comes from a completely different source. The power comes from a very specific application of *truth* as it is realized through the discipline of good playwriting.

Telling the Truth

Some may say, "But the Four Spiritual Laws and John 3:16 *are* true." Yes, agreed. Just as it may also be true that a certain detergent will get your clothes whiter or a certain mouthwash will make your breath mintier or a myriad of other commercial products will make you a cleaner, more hygienically acceptable person.

But the power of drama is not contained in an objective truth coldly dispensed by contrived cardboard characters who have walked through a story thinly disguised to bring us to the point where we, the audience, will hear that truth. That's not drama—that's a commercial. We've merely replaced the detergent with Christ.

The best minds on Madison Avenue know that unless a commercial is incredibly funny, clever, or informative, most people instinctively rebel against it. People rebel against the contrivance of commercial characters who are merely puppets placed in a superficial situation to sell a product. One could argue that that's how the "truth" of the gospel appears to those who aren't Christians, especially when it isn't framed in a plausible, compelling story with realistic characters and dialogue. The audience suspects that they're not really being told the truth—they're merely being sold something.

And that's the difference between art and propaganda, or art and commercials. Art must not merely inform but open up our hearts and imaginations.

Writer Murray Watts gets to the heart of the issue of truth in his book *Christianity and the Theatre*. There he laments well-meaning Christians who would forever constrain drama in the church to commercials for Christ. He presents an environment where reality and the deepest, most heartfelt (yes, even controversial) issues are never dealt with because they may be "seen as damaging to a successful public relations campaign for God." He then raises an important question:

> But if Christian artists do not speak the truth at all times, especially when it is most costly to themselves and their own self-esteem, how can they be trusted to speak the truth when literally proclaiming the gospel of Christ? If artists censor their imagination and restrict their work to acceptable subjects, then they enter a conspiracy against the audience. Experience shows that most people have sensitive noses for such deceptions. They can sniff out a charlatan. They will recognize, in due course, the difference between the cult-member with the glazed eyes and rehearsed speeches, and the men and women who offer their very own selves. This was St. Paul's defini-

tion of his ministry: "we offered not only the gospel, but our own selves." The Christian artist can do no less. For better or worse, he must have freedom to open his heart.[5]

The Ring of Truth

When J. B. Phillips translated the New Testament into modern English, he wrote about the process in *Ring of Truth,* so-named because he was delighted to find that the words of Scripture resonated deep within him, touching an "inner truth" that he recognized in part intuitively and in part from personal experience.[6]

The ring of truth in a play is the truth about your humanity that resonates *within* the humanity of your audience. It engages the heart, mind, and soul. How? By putting forward deep theology or philosophy? Hardly. The best plays are about humanity—people—first and foremost.

Yes, there *should* be a message. You as a playwright should know what you believe and what you hope to communicate. Esteemed professor and author Louis Catron makes it very clear in the first chapter of *The Elements of Playwriting* that being a playwright involves not only identifying your beliefs but organizing them as well.[7] However, your message, theology and philosophy should be found *within* your story, behind the dialogue and actions of your characters. To horribly paraphrase C. S. Lewis, your message should seem invisible until it bubbles to the top as your play comes to a boil.

God himself recognized this very human need for human interaction, sending His Son as a man of flesh and blood and not as some abstract idea.

In his seminars on writing, best-selling author Philip Yancey teaches one "universal": writing works best when it accurately reflects the question "What is a human being?"

For dramatists, the answer is realized through characters. They should be complex, intellectual, emotional, and spiritual. They are sensory beings caught in time and space who experience love and hatred, compassion and anger, curiosity and complacency . . . the list goes on and on.

But in that list, as realized through your characters, your audience should experience *the ring of truth.*

You'll see that phrase used again and again in this book as we examine stories, character and dialogue. We will ask: Do they have the *ring of truth* for you and, of equal importance, your audience? If you can answer confidently that they do, then you're well on your way to writing a play that won't merely be a commercial for Christ, but a genuine representation of the truth.

A Good Story Well Told

So what does all this have to do with art and craft? Plenty. It is *art* that brings truth to the forefront of any creative work and *craft* that makes it accessible.

Robert McKee, a popular lecturer on writing for film, has defined the best scripts from Hollywood as simply "good stories well told." A "good story," he says, is the *expression;* "well told" is the *craft.*

Let's turn the tables for a moment. It often happens that a writer may have an artistic grasp on his writing but not on the craftsmanship. There are Christians who want to write but resist the training that will aid them in their writing. "The Lord gave it to me," they are heard to say. If asked whether they've taken any writing courses or had their work critiqued by a professional, they simply say, "Nope. The Lord gave it to me." And, as if to prove it, they tell me how the folks in their churches wept openly when their plays were performed or how people raced down the aisle to accept Jesus at the altar or collapsed right where they were under the burden of their convicted spirits. All as a result of their scripts.

Yet, if you actually *read* the scripts, it's easy to wonder how the Creator of the universe; the God of Abraham, Isaac, and Jacob; the Author of the Psalms; the Spirit behind all that is good and true . . . could write so terribly.

Yes, God can take our feeblest creative outpourings and work such a miracle that lives are drawn to Him. The Bible is full of examples where God worked *in spite of* human effort. But we should never intentionally write anything so second-rate that God has to rescue it. We must give Him our very best—with no less preparation, skill, or craftsmanship than we would expect from a doctor who is about to operate on us.

On this subject, British playwright Nigel Forde conjures the image of a well-intentioned engineer who builds a bridge that collapses and kills thousands; or the novice Christian who, scalpel in hand, approaches a sick member of the congregation and says, "Don't worry, I've *prayed* about it."[8]

Yet, how often do we take that approach to the arts in our churches? Imagine this: a soloist stands up on a Sunday morning and sings a beautifully written song—missing half the notes. The congregation smiles pleasantly and even commends the singer on a job well done after the service. They want to be encouraging. They don't want to criticize. They think to themselves, "But he's a good boy, he means well." But, unfortunately, that singer confuses the responses of a sympathetic audience with a mandate to "use his talent for the Lord." Without proper, loving correction and training, our misguided singer goes on to other venues, only to look foolish and untalented, perhaps even giving up singing forever because he feels disillusioned and bitter.

It happens all the time.

It happens when Christians wander into the secular market with mediocre work, then wonder why they aren't taken seriously. ("Obviously they're persecuting us because we're Christians," they mope.)

We should never be critical for criticism's sake. But how else will so-called Christian arts get past the reputation of being second rate if we don't *demand of ourselves* to meet the very highest standards in what we do?

Christian vs. Secular

Perhaps part of the problem rests in the idea that there is such a thing as *Christian* art. Are there really differences between Christian and secular when it comes to art?

Well, yes. There *is* a difference between Christian and secular. But that difference comes from *perspective* and worldview, not anything within the art or craft itself. A well-written play is a well-written play regardless of its perspective.

But does *Christian* art exist?

Apart from the use of the phrase by marketers to quickly identify products or the consumers who buy those products, it's hard to imagine how the noun *Christian* became an adjective.

Media analyst and writer Ted Baehr makes the case quite well:

> It would be a great breakthrough if communicators would refrain from using the word Christian as an adjective and limit its use to the way in which the early church and the Romans used it, as a noun. In the Book of the Acts of the Apostles, a Christian is a person who confesses and follows Jesus Christ. Paul is a Christian who makes tents; however, the tents that Paul makes are not "Christian" tents.
>
> If we restricted the use of "Christian," we would no longer be confused by "Christian" art and media. Instead, we would have Christians who made a work of art, for example, or created a televi-

sion program. The work of art or the television program may or may not communicate the Gospel of Jesus Christ. If we evaluated the art as art, the television program as a program, and the tent as a tent (including any Gospel messages woven into the fabric), we would be delivered from worshiping the thing as a sacred object set apart by the use of "Christian" as an adjective.[9]

A number of years ago, W. H. Auden considered this issue and concluded that "there can no more be a 'Christian' art than there can be a Christian science or a Christian diet. There can only be a Christian spirit in which an artist, a scientist, does or does not work. A painting of the crucifixion is not necessarily more Christian in spirit than a still life, and may very well be less."[10]

"It is a mistake to believe that there are two different sorts of art: Christian art and everybody else's art," adds Nigel Forde.[11]

One has to wonder by what criteria anything we do can be defined as Christian. If, as a Christian, one constructs a dresser—is it a Christian dresser? Can a baker who is a Christian make Christian bread? Can a surgeon who is a Christian do Christian heart surgery? Christian street cleaners . . . Christian mechanics . . . Christian architects . . . Christian telephone operators . . . the list goes on and on.

Of course, we would hope that these jobs are filled by Christians who are doing their absolute best at them. But one shouldn't be so naive as to assume that only a Christian could do them well or that their work is somehow blessed over and above an atheist's attempts at baking bread or street cleaning or the like.

Perhaps it's splitting hairs. For the majority of people, using the term *Christian* in front of the place where they buy their books or to identify certain movies or frozen dinners or hair spray may simply be an act of convenience. It's an easy label to clarify expectations.

Labels and debates aside, there are *universal* elements to be found in "good stories well told" as plays. The true difference between Christian and secular plays isn't in the elements themselves but in the person who mixes the elements together and in the prayer that goes with the mixing.

EXERCISES

1. Write the definitive commercial for Christianity.

2. Consider a modern play—*A Streetcar Named Desire, Glengarry Glen Ross,* or *The Odd Couple,* as three examples—and write out how you would "Christianize" it. What would you do to the characters? The ending? The overriding theme?

3. Begin a writer's journal. In it, write down in simple declarative sentences the 10 most important things you believe—20, if you can manage it.

4. Think of people in real life that you admire. What qualities draw you to them? Think of characters in plays, movies, and books that you like. Detail what you like about them.

5. Take the negative angle on Question 4. Detail the things you *don't* like in real people and in characters you've seen.

6. Make a list of your favorite plays. Detail *why* you liked them.

TWO

The Elements of a Play (and from Whence They Come)

A play is a structured and unified story, comic or dramatic, complete in itself with a beginning, middle and end, that expresses the playwright's passion and vision of life, shows unfolding conflict that builds to a climax, and deals with dimensional lifelike humans who have strong emotions, needs and objectives that motivate them to take action. It is constructed with a plausible and probable series of events, written to be performed and therefore told with speeches and actions plus silences and inactions, projected by actors from a stage to an audience that is made to believe the events are happening as they watch.

—Louis Catron[12]

When all is said and done, a play consists of three basic yet intricately bound elements. A *good story* with *good characters* and *good dialogue*. The glue that holds those three elements together is *conflict*. Mess around with any one of those elements—try to enhance one by diminishing another (or any combination thereof)—and you'll have a weak play.

It's worth pointing out that most storytelling mediums—novels or films—consist of those same elements. That's why you need to be certain that it's a *play* you want to write.

For example, many plays in the Christian arena are really only sermons put on a stage. One never has a sense of real characters moving through real situations. They're simply mouthpieces for the author, expressing ideas to each other in a theatrical medium. Traditionally, such plays are called closet dramas because they're meant to be read and discussed, not performed. Plato's *Dialogues* is an example of a closet drama. Many others have been created throughout history. Unfortunately, there are a lot of well-meaning writers who want to communicate Christian values the same way. Worse, they don't realize that they've created an unperformable closet drama instead of a fully fleshed-out *play*.

Another example is when the forward movement of your story is held back by a lot of narration, internal analysis, or exposition by your character (or characters). If so, you may be writing a *novel* rather than a play.

Or if your play seems to contain a lot of short scenes in a lot of different locations while it jumps to different points in time quickly, then you may be writing a *film*.

Make sure your story is appropriate for the *stage* and not better suited to another form.

What Is Appropriate for the Stage?

What the page is to a novel, the canvas to a painting, film to a movie —the stage is to your play.

There on the stage, living and breathing actors and actresses will perform for a living and breathing audience—establishing an intimacy no other medium can create. It is a representation of life being played out before the audience's eyes. And, like life, every moment is instantly lost to the next moment. All action moves forward. There's no point where a member of the audience can stop the play like a videotape and rewind it to see what he or she missed. There's no flipping a few pages back to double-check the information. There's no asking the performers to wait—like putting a book down for a moment—so the audience can pause to think about what was just said or done. Each moment comes and goes very quickly.

For that reason, you (the playwright) must be sensitive, shrewd, and uncanny in how your play unfolds before the audience. You can't move too fast or too slow. Try to be too clever and the audience will get hung up on the cleverness. Try to shock and the audience will be so stunned that whatever you've written for the next 10 minutes will be wasted.

Bernard Grebanier notes in *Playwriting: How to Write for the Theater* that in a scene containing two people there are actually *three* present. Romeo may be speaking to Juliet, but his words go to her via the audience. Juliet's response goes to Romeo via the audience. Leave your audience out of the equation, and you may as well forget about writing a play. Novelists don't sit with every reader who opens their books. Filmmakers —even painters—do not face the dynamic of a sea of live faces sitting before them, watching and waiting. Drama for the stage is the one art form that *demands* an audience be present.

That's what separates a work written for the stage from works written for other forms of media. It is live; it is life.

But a Play Is Not Reality

Your play is not reality. It is a *representation* of reality—a metaphor, an allegory, an illusion that is bigger than life. As a writer, you will create a *perceived* reality. It's a reality where every move, every utterance must have meaning. There are no wasted moments. Where true reality is often too boring or too mundane to hold audience interest, the reality you create has the constant forward movement of conflict, a heightening of tension. It is time through a prism, emotions under a magnifying glass, ideas wrapped in a disguise of flesh and blood.

Types of Plays to Consider

One choice you'll ultimately make in determining your "reality" will be the *type* of play your reality operates within. Though these types can intermingle in a variety of ways, here are the basics:

Tragedy: a serious play where your hero—generally a sympathetic character—struggles against great obstacles but ultimately loses (often by death).

Drama: a serious play where your hero struggles against great obstacles and may win or, at the very least, learn or change in such a way that winning isn't necessary.

Melodrama: a serious play with a happy ending that is often sensational in its plot, containing artificially motivated characters who use a lot of physical action, contrived conflict, and suspense. For some reason, writers for the Christian market write in this genre—whether they mean to or not.

Comedy: a humorous play where your hero struggles against obstacles but ultimately wins. In *high comedy* (or *comedy of manners*), your characters and setting are upper-class socially and your humor depends on verbal wit. *Low comedy* or *farce* depends less on verbal wit and more on physical actions with ridiculous situations and surprise twists. *Tragicomedy* brings together aspects of both tragedy and comedy, often a tragic situation with comic devices.

These are simplistic definitions, of course, and don't cover the entire range of theatrical expression.

As is true for all the elements of your play, whatever your genre, you should stay *true* to it throughout. It is part of the *universe* you've created—the perceived reality you've established for your audience. You must never betray them by betraying the ground rules you've set up. Imagine a serious play where the climax is the moment when Lazarus is called back from the grave by Jesus. Lazarus steps out of the dark tomb wearing top hat and tails, dances the watusi, and is then zapped into oblivion by men in space suits. Absurd? Yes. So what would your audience think if, up to that point, you gave no hint that you were once the head writer for Monty Python movies?

Would it be right to do a play about a werewolf who is healed after he becomes a Christian?

Would it be a good mix to have your hero—a truck driver in the Eugene O'Neill mold—reach his greatest moment of crisis, only to be saved by the ghost of Abraham Lincoln speaking like a character from a Neil Simon play?

Louis Catron writes that our ideas must be "possible, plausible and probable."[13]

Should You Write a Sketch, a One-Act, or Full-Length Play?

You will likely wonder at some point whether your idea should be written as a sketch, a one-act play, or a full-length (two- or three-act) play. Hard-and-fast definitions are difficult to come by, but tradition helps us understand the differences.

A sketch sticks to one idea or conclusion, usually in one scene set in one place. It can last from a minute up to 20 or 30 minutes.

A one-act often contains one idea or situation caught in a particular point of time that's played out in more than one scene. One-acts are sometimes between 20 to 60 minutes long.

A full-length play (two or three acts), can last 90 minutes to over two hours. The plot and characters are far more complex than you'd find in a one-act or a sketch, since you'll have more time to explore them.

Choosing the best format for your play depends entirely on your idea. Some ideas better suited for one-acts have been stretched mercilessly into full-length plays. (Rarely does the opposite happen, since most writers like to say *more*—whether they need to or not.)

In making your decision, it may be helpful to ask yourself some basic questions—particularly since you're likely writing for a church rather than a community theatre or Broadway. It's a simple *who, what, how, when and where* approach.

Who are you writing to? (Audience)

What are you trying to say? (Theme)

How are you going to say it? (Tragedy? Comedy?)

When and where will it be said? (In church, in a morning service, at an informal talent night? etc.)

Why should anyone care? (Something *every* playwright needs to be concerned about.)

Answering these questions accurately will help you make the correct decision for what you're going to write.

So . . . What Is a Play?

As stated already, a play is a stageworthy combination of a good story with good characters and good dialogue in equal measure. At the heart of those elements is conflict: opposing desires, opposing forces, opposing personalities, opposing motives, opposing everything—but carefully constructed to bring conflict to a point of climax and resolution.

Theme and Premise

Your *theme* is the subtle "message" that "bubbles" to the top as your play comes to a boil. It's your governing idea that pervades your plot and your characters. It's *what you believe*—about people, the world, God. Yet your theme should be "an interpretation of life, not a lecture upon it,"[14] as Grebanier says.

Your *premise* is the overriding situation with a beginning, a middle, and an end. This is where your theme comes to life in the characters you've chosen, the situation in which you've placed them, and the action they take in response to their situation.

For example, if your theme is that, no matter what, you can't run away from God, then your premise may be the story of a man who is told by God to preach to an enemy nation, but catches a boat heading in the opposite direction. You may never hear a character actually *say* "Guess what? You can't run away from God." But through the character of Jonah and the sailors, their action (Jonah runs, the sailors throw him overboard), and dialogue (Captain of the Ship: "You were trying to do *what*? Are you crazy, Jonah? Why did you bring this calamity on us?") we realize the theme. And it's accomplished through a premise with a beginning, a middle, and an end.

The Elements of Conflict

You cannot have a good story, good characters, or good dialogue without conflict. Conflict drives your story forward. Conflict *proves* character—gives character multidimensions—as we witness how they act and what they say in the face of conflict. Your character may say he is a coward and truly believe it, but the conflict may prove otherwise. Or Peter, for example, who swore to stand bravely by Jesus to the end, but did the opposite when the conflict truly came.

And just as we've already determined that humans care mostly about humans, the best conflict arises out of very human characters.

Your Protagonist

The classic plays utilize the most basic rule: You have *one* protagonist who wants something but is hindered by or at odds with an antagonist of equal or greater strength.

Think back to your high school English class for the kinds of conflicts the classic stories presented: Man vs. Man (or Society), Man vs. Himself, Man vs. Nature, Man vs. God.

Man vs. Man: David against Goliath. Or, in the case of Man vs. Society, Elijah against fallen Israel, Jesus against legalistic religious leaders.

Man vs. Himself: Peter follows Jesus against his better sense, then denies Jesus against his greater desire. Or the apostle Paul lives out his frustration of not doing the things he ought to do, and doing the things he ought not to do.

Man vs. Nature: The story of Noah.

Man vs. God: The story of Jonah. All of us.

Who is this "Man"? He or she is your protagonist. He or she needs to be sympathetically human in attributes—even if not literally human. Winnie-the-Pooh or Peter Rabbit are two examples of nonhumans who are *very* human anyway. Why *sympathetically* human? Successful playwrights know that there must be a connection between the protagonist and the audience. There must be some redeeming attribute, something people can relate to—a point of identification—or the audience won't care to sit and watch for two hours. We relate to David, though few of us have ever struck down a giant or been chased by a mad king. We understand how Peter felt after denying Christ. We identify with Jonah's desire to escape. We appreciate Noah's struggle to keep his family and animals alive on the ark while the waters engulfed the earth.

But, unlike many of us, your protagonist must *want* something—and must know exactly what that something is. Otherwise there's no potential for conflict.

Your Antagonist

Your antagonist doesn't have to have human attributes but certainly must be an equal or better match for your protagonist. If your antagonist is overtly weaker than your protagonist, then there really isn't a conflict. If compromise is possible, there isn't a conflict. If victory by one side or the other is readily available, there isn't a conflict.

Goliath makes a wonderful antagonist because he was bigger and more powerful than David. Jezebel makes a wonderful antagonist because she had the authority of the crown on her side against Elijah.

As a side note: two dangers exist with many stories (plays or otherwise) written from a Christian viewpoint. One is that the antagonist is stereotypically evil—no real motivation, no multifaceted personality—just a bad guy.

The other danger is the opposite extreme: when the antagonist actually comes off more appealing than the protagonist. Somehow the antagonist seems more clever, more in control, more charming . . . in other words, the antagonist has more of the attributes we *wish* we had. This sometimes happens because the playwright spends more time fleshing out the dimensions of the antagonist's character while the protagonist remains simplistically "good." This is a more noticeable danger when writing programs for children. Your antagonist becomes more of an appealing role model than your protagonist.

Dialogue

Dialogue is a reflection of the multidimensional character as the character works through conflict. It encompasses what we as the audience need to know but only when we need to know it. It should ring true to who the character is (or wants to be) while driving the story forward. Or, to put it simply: no wasted words. Just as every action must be motivated by a driving force, every word must be motivated. Otherwise, why bother putting it in?

The Result

Your protagonist wants something and your antagonist is keeping him from getting it. This basic conflict builds—tension winds tighter, the stakes increase, the risks get riskier—leading us to an irreversible crisis, the climax, which ultimately provides a satisfying conclusion. *That's* what makes a good play.

EXERCISES

1. Think about, then write out, the various conflicts you've experienced in your own life. Who is the protagonist? Who is the antagonist? What exactly is the conflict? Are there any elements in the conflict that might make a good sketch, one-act, or play?

2. Make a list of things that people want. Move from the abstract (happiness) to the specific (a particular house in a particular neighborhood). In a column next to that list, write down the things people do to *get* what they want.

3. Think about your favorite Bible stories. How would you adapt them for stage? What scenes would you keep? What scenes would you delete? How would you consolidate scenes, characters, and action to make the story stageworthy?

4. Think about a play you've been wanting to write (or are currently writing). Minimize the entire idea to a single sentence that includes your protagonist, your antagonist, and the conflict.

5. Think about your play from Question 4. How would it be different if you made it a melodrama? A tragedy? A comedy? A farce?

---— THREE ——

Getting Started

When I am asked where I get my ideas from I know, first of all, that the questioner has never written anything himself or he would not ask such a daft question. Secondly, I know that an honest answer is going to disappoint him or her. Somehow it always does. What such people want, if they are honest, is a magical solution.

—Nigel Forde[15]

Getting started on your play may well be the hardest part of the process. "What should I write about?" is the first choice you have to make—and it can become a daunting, unanswerable monster if you don't take a few steps back from it and remember a couple of things.

Few Instant Plays

Don't expect the entire play to rush at you the instant you think you've hit on an idea. On rare occasions, that may happen. You have an idea and suddenly you know exactly what the beginning, the middle, and the end are. But those are *very* rare occasions. More often than not, you'll experience what Catron calls the "search, exploration and discovery" process. You search for what seems to be a good idea. Then you explore that idea—by chasing characters and plot lines down different avenues and alleyways to see where they lead. Through discovery, you'll reach dead ends and have to retrace your steps, or you may find your way to an entirely different neighborhood that bears little resemblance to the one in which you started.

Whatever happens, wherever your idea leads, don't think you've failed or are "less than creative" simply because it doesn't all click into place in an instant. Plan now to persevere in the work and the choices that wait ahead.

By the way, there's great value in taking copious notes on your "journey" through ideas—even if they seem to lead nowhere. Many great stories and plays were unintentionally discovered while running down the alley of an entirely *different* idea. Note it, file it. It may seem useless now, but it could prove invaluable much later.

Experience Counts, but Isn't Everything

I remember being told in school to "write about what you know or have experienced." This is decent advice, but subject to misinterpretation if taken literally. By the letter of that law, a man couldn't write from a woman's perspective (or vice versa), one who didn't have children couldn't write about parents, young about the aged, laymen about pastors, present-day writers about other points of history—and no one could ever write about death. The list goes on. By that rule, we are limited to our own little worlds and the kinds of people contained in them.

Instead, what we "know" or have "experienced" should really mean: all we know, have experienced, seen, read, heard, or dreamed about thrown into our remarkable imaginations to be used, pondered, blended, mixed, twisted, turned, and processed for whatever is appropriate for our idea.

Some of the best writing I've ever done was for plays that took place entirely outside of my own experience; situations where I had to "put myself in someone else's shoes" to try to understand the person's feelings or thoughts. (Of course, that brings with it the higher demand for it to ring true, particularly for those who *have* experienced whatever I've written about.)

Starting Points: Theme and Premise

Your theme and premise are, in some respects, the two feet you use for the race ahead. You can start with one or the other—there's no guaranteed rule on the subject. Sometimes a play may be born out of an overriding idea (your theme). You may be thinking about honesty, integrity, passion, hope—or the negatives of those concepts. Or you may be pondering what your story is about—a situation or series of events or characters in situations and what happens (your premise). Sometimes both will come together. Other times they may emerge out of each other. Or they may be dictated to you by a higher authority (like those times when you're asked to do a play to supplement a series of sermons the pastor is preaching).

Regardless of which foot takes the first step, you'll still have to move ahead to see where it leads—even if it's all the way back to the beginning.

So, where do those themes and premises come from? Some playwrights play the What If? game.

What if a pastor suddenly discovered that his best friend—the head deacon (or elder) of the church—was lobbying to have him dismissed? (A situation-based start.)

What if a meek young man who lived in his seemingly perfect father's shadow his whole life suddenly found out some dark secrets about his father after Dad died? (A character-based situation.)

What if you put a certain type of character—weak, strong, greedy, worried—into that character's worst nightmare, played out that worst fear, and came face-to-face with a situation that would prove or break him or her? (Character and situation.)

Pose a situation or a particular type of character in a situation then ask, "What if?"

Theme starters may be: What is truth? What are the consequences of greed? What does it mean to carry one's cross—even to death? What is the folly of "following the world"?

The questions are endless. The answers may come as you find your germinal idea then begin to mix and match it with the characters and situations playing them out. This can only happen as you ask yourself what you would do in those situations, what others would do, what *ought* to be done.

Here are other ways to come up with ideas:

On Your Own

Observe. Go to a shopping center, airport, museum, or other public place and watch the people who go by. Observe the way they relate to each other, the minidramas that sometimes unfold as a mother tries to deal with a restless baby or an annoyed wife chastises her husband for buying some unnecessary item or greetings between friends or good-byes or . . . Most public places have a myriad of "performances" going on if you're astute enough to notice them.

Read. The Bible, novels (classics and modern—and *not* only Christian), plays . . . Give yourself time to absorb, ponder, and filter other people's ideas and views.

Go to plays. Professional productions, community theatre, amateur, high school . . . whatever. Go, watch, observe, take notes, and remember what it is about live drama that makes it so remarkable. Even the most awful performances can be inspiring.

Keep a journal. Quickly note or chronicle in detail your observations, thoughts, or activities in a day. Jot down stories you've heard or character traits of people you've met (or have known).

Personal experience. In your journal or as you think of ideas for plays, think back on your own personal experiences—events that captured your imagination as a child or as an adult.

Personal encounters. Think of people you know and what became of them.

Personal beliefs. It can be a very interesting exercise to sit down and list what you *truly* believe—about yourself, your family and friends, life, God, church, etc.—in positive and negative ways. (This can also be a frightening exercise if you discover that you don't really believe many things you *assumed* you believe.)

Objective beliefs. Think of spiritual truths and values; the consequences of our human failings and sin; the nobility of being—what we do *right;* social or church issues (what kills a church? My film noir play *Case of the Frozen Saints* tried to answer that question within a comic murder-mystery detective genre); high ideals that don't line up with reality (*Pete's Garage*, a teen play I wrote for Baker's plays)—the old formula of someone getting a wrong idea, playing it out comically or tragically, then learning how to do it right.

Biblical stories. Not only a straight stage presentation, but an adaptation that might update the story of, say, Jonah (a prophet on the run). Or Samson (modernized—an industrial giant who slays the competition, only to be undone by his vanity and foolishness). Use the basic themes and story lines of the biblical story, but place them in an unexpected time period or setting. (Another example: one of the best versions I've ever seen of Shakespeare's *Richard III* was set in Nazi Germany.)

Another way to adapt Bible stories, by the way, is to take the *Ben-Hur* approach. Create a second, unfamiliar story to parallel the main biblical story. That way, while your audience may think they know how the Bible story will work out, they will be held in suspense until the fictional story climaxes.

A word or a phrase. For me, *Catacombs* started as just the word itself, and then free association led to the image of first-century Christians in hiding during the Roman persecution, which led to an image of ruins—church ruins, in particular—a run-down church somewhere, which then connected with the idea of a modern period of persecution where Christians on the run hide out in an abandoned church in the mountains.

With Others

If you have a group of writers or actors you regularly see or work with, you may want to use them as a resource for brainstorming. Ways to do this include sitting around a table or in a casual setting and tape-recording the proceedings. Remember, though, the *Golden Rule* of brainstorming: all suggestions are valid. It's unkind and unproductive to shoot down or make fun of *any* idea.

Discuss topics, settings and characters—playing the What If? game. Use improvisation. If your friends are actors, ask them to improvise some of the scenes and ideas.

And Then . . .

Whether you work alone or with someone else, be sure to write down all your ideas. Don't try to make a judgment about whether they're good or bad immediately. Mull over them for awhile. Play the What If? game. If one leaps out at you, grab it (or chase after it, as the case may be). File the rest for another brainstorming day.

Once You've Made a Choice

If you have settled on an idea, try to summarize it in a couple of paragraphs. *My play is about . . .* or *Once upon a time . . .* or anything that gets your pen moving.

Take a look at the idea again, and ask some basic questions. Is there solid conflict in your story? Who is your protagonist? Who is your antagonist? Are their characters equally matched in determination, motivation, and force of will? Is one stronger than the other? In other words, are your characters involved in a solid conflict? To whom (which character) does the play belong? Is it a "talky" play, or are your characters and plot realized through action? Do you know where the play will begin? What happens in the middle? What is the climax? Where will the play end? Where is it set (time and place)?

Outlining Your Choice

To outline or not to outline? For many, *that's* the question. I have read interviews with successful playwrights who don't or who refuse to outline. They know in their heads where they're going with an idea and don't need to write it down beforehand. Or they choose to "make it up as they go along," allowing their creativity to guide them along.

While that sounds good in theory (and I reluctantly confess that I've written a few plays that way), I suspect that those playwrights have wonderful instincts and have mastered many of the basic skills of storytelling. They know intuitively whether or not they're on the right trail—whether the play is working *while* they're writing it and if the audience will be satisfied with how it turns out.

I'll also confess that outlining has, on occasion, spoiled the writing; as if in writing a detailed outline I feel like I've already written the play and lost interest. (At this moment, I can think of one play that I detailed to the nth degree and still haven't gotten around to writing.)

On the positive side, outlining your idea is helpful for answering many of the questions asked earlier and for realizing the true potential of your characters and plot. It's an informal road map of where the many roads are leading you. Outlining is beneficial for keeping track of character and plot details. It's a form of shorthand to remind you of smaller or secondary ideas.

Outlines can also be as sketchy or as detailed as you want. Sometimes just a heading of "Act One, Scene One" with one sentence of what happens will do the job. Other times you may need a paragraph (or two or three . . .) just to map out what happens.

Outlining can save you from unnecessary work. You may *think* you know where your play is going and how it will get there, but it's an awful feeling to reach a point in the actual writing of the play when you discover that you missed an important plot turn or came up against something implausible or a character action that doesn't make sense and have to backtrack through everything to fix it. An outline can give you advance notice of potential problems.

However, outlines are just the *rough* guides, not written in concrete, and shouldn't be confused with the finished play. It's the pencil sketch before the painting, the Polaroid before the camera shot, the early blocking before the set is built. There are twists and turns that can be discovered or worked out only in the writing of the play itself. Some things you simply can't know until you get there.

In conclusion, I strongly suggest outlining your play before you get started—unless you're Neil Simon or Arthur Miller—in which case you probably won't need my suggestion anyway.

EXERCISES

1. Write down a word or a phrase, then play a game of association with it. For example, I remember playing around with a phrase from the Lord's Prayer—*forgive us our trespasses*—turning it into *forgive us our trucks passing*. That led me to an idea about a church sitting next to a busy highway, like an old truck stop diner with a garage. I thought

about the image of a garage, thinking more along the lines of a garage at home and how I used to play in one as a kid. This led me further on to the idea of a group of kids playing "church" in a garage. Somehow I connected that thought with a period of rebellion I went through at my church when, as a teenager, I constantly complained that the church wasn't all that Christ wanted it to be. A what if? emerged. *What if a group of young people complain to their pastor about how bad the church is . . . and he challenges them to "start their own church"?* And that's how a little one-act play called *The First Church of Pete's Garage* came about.

2. Think of many heartfelt experiences people have during the normal course of life: dealing with a bully at school, a first kiss, the birth of a baby, the death of a loved one, struggles with getting a job, graduation from high school, breaking off a relationship for some reason, a time when one feels jealous or extremely happy or at odds with the world. The list goes on and on. *Pap's Place*, a play of mine, began when a friend suggested I write something about Alzheimer's disease and the effect it has on a family. In time, the idea metamorphosized into the many changes a family experiences as members grow old, lose jobs, etc. It was originally written for the Jeremiah People touring group, so the parameters of the play—the number of characters—were determined even before I wrote: I needed to write for three lead males (with one secondary character to be played by the group's bus driver) and two females. It's a decent example of things you may need to consider if you're writing specifically for your own church group.

3. Get some file cards and put them into three piles. Name one pile "Character," the next "Situation," and the final "Theme." On the "Character" cards, brainstorm different types of characters, personality traits, motivations, etc. (one per card is best). After that, move to the "Situation" pile and think through as many situations (preferably conflicts) as you can (again, one per card). And finish doing the same with the "Theme" pile. On a large table, begin to mix and match the characters with the situations and the themes . . . and see where they lead.

4. Assume we're following the old rule to "write only what you know." Make a list of the 10 most influential experiences you've had in your life. Then outline each experience into a story with a beginning, a middle, and an end. If applicable, consider who the protagonist was? The antagonist? The conflict?

5. Play the What If? game, making a list of what if? situations.

6. Think (or go back to your writer's journal) of your answers to Questions 4 and 5 in chapter 1. Now use your answers as themes for ideas.

——— FOUR ———

Your Story

A story must be exceptional enough to justify its telling.
—Thomas Hardy, Notebook Entry

Plots are no more exhausted than men are. Every man is a new creation, and combinations are simply endless.
—Charles Dudley Warner, "Sixth Study"

I think you must remember that a writer is a simple-minded person to begin with and go on that basis. He's not a great mind, he's not a great thinker, he's not a great philosopher, he's a story-teller.
—Erskine Caldwell, *The Atlantic Monthly*

"Once upon a time . . ." isn't such a bad place to start.
—Paul McCusker, this very page

Let's pause for a moment to consider your story—your plot—the premise upon which everything in your play is dependent. Even before you begin, what do we know about it?

First, it should have a beginning, a middle, and an end.

The Beginning

How does your play start? Do you introduce a few of the characters, explain their backgrounds, establish the setting, then get things moving?

Hopefully not.

The best plays begin with an *inciting incident*—something that happened before the play began or happens right then and there. Get your audience into the play *right away.* Hook them into your story, and don't let them go until the final curtain.

"In the beginning, God created the heavens and the earth" (Genesis).

Hamlet's father was murdered *(Hamlet).*

A pompous, arrogant professor bets that he can change a lower-class woman into a high-class lady (*Pygmalion* or the musical *My Fair Lady*).

A band of outlaw Christians find a mysterious stranger in the woods outside of the mountain church where they are hiding (*Catacombs*).

God tells Jonah to preach to a rival nation called Nineveh (*Jonah*).

The word *drama* comes from the Greek *dran*, meaning "to do." Drama is movement. It is action. So start your play at a *point* of *action*. Save the background information—or *exposition*—for when it's really needed.

I can confess from personal experience that too often I've started my plays with more set-up than was needed. I felt obligated to say everything there was to say and *then* start the action. With hindsight, I can now look at those plays and admit I would've been better off starting in the *middle* of the first scene—when things really start to happen—and simply cut or minimize what came before.

Yet that doesn't mean you're free from establishing your characters, the situation/conflict, environment, and mood. Those elements must be introduced to your audience. But think carefully how you can let them be seen through *action* (by action, I also mean *conflict*) and not through the kind of exposition often seen in farces (or Christian drama) where two characters—usually servants of some sort—enter the stage and have a ridiculously contrived chat about the principal characters and the situation to come. Older plays used a chorus. Modern plays have used things like radios, televisions, telephones, etc.

Any exposition should be hidden in casual, conversational lines and reactions and should quickly bring the audience to the important questions of your play: what does your protagonist want, how will he get it, *will* he get it? (For many, this last question is called the major dramatic question and is the clothesline upon which your literary laundry is hung.) We'll talk more about exposition in the chapter on dialogue.

Your beginning may also contain the *foreshadowing* of things to come: a mood or emotion, a reference to an approaching storm, a physical item like a letter opener or gun or Bible that becomes important later, a character trait or flaw that seems incidental initially but becomes vital later.

The Middle

Your plot's middle is the longest (in percentage of time and number of pages) and likely the most complex part of your play. There, you'll create the *rising action* of your story. Rising action increases the tension as consequences are played out by the protagonist and antagonist, which, in turn, create *new* difficulties and consequences, resulting in change, turning points, reversals, obstacles—and ultimately leading to a climactic crisis point.

And so you now rightfully ask, "What did he say?"

Let's consider the story of Jonah as example. If the beginning of the story—the inciting incident—is God telling Jonah to go to Nineveh, then the middle is what becomes of him after that. Will he go to Nineveh? No. What does he do? He heads in the other direction. How? He takes a boat, perhaps using his influence as a well-known prophet to get a stateroom. Then what? God lets loose a hurricane that threatens the ship. Does Jonah die as a result? No. The sailors on the ship fearfully but valiantly fight for control while Jonah sleeps (or hides) below deck. Then what? Knowing that Jonah is a prophet, the captain seeks out Jonah to call to his God for help. Unbeknownst to the captain, this is the *last* thing Jonah wants to do. So Jonah refuses. The captain returns to his men and they superstitiously cast lots to determine who is to blame for this calamity. The lot falls to Jonah, and the sailors ask him why God is trying to destroy the ship. Jonah explains. The sailors are horrified and demand to know what they can do to save their lives. Jonah tells them to throw him overboard. They refuse and try other alternatives—rowing back to shore, etc. Nothing works. Finally, they throw Jonah overboard.

And then what . . . ?

It's a wonderful story, complete with twists, reversals, and complications. If you allow yourself to crawl into Jonah's skin and play out the doubts, confusion, and terror of the sailors, you'll find that it's full of humanity. Imagine how the captain must feel to go to the prophet, believing him to be the ship's only hope, to find that he's the *cause* of the problem. Imagine how Jonah felt to realize that God was chasing after him. Imagine . . .

This is the middle of your play. The consequences of your inciting incident get played out. The goal of your protagonist is explored.

Goals

The best plays establish that your character wants something, then works out the question will he or she get what he or she wants? Perhaps Jonah wants a peaceful, carefree life, which seems to be disrupted by a command from God. His goal is then to escape from God, where he'll resume his peaceful, carefree life somewhere else. Will he succeed?

A trait of the most successful stories is to detail how far the protagonist gets pushed to get what he wants. How much will he risk? Initially, your character wants something and will do the easiest thing to get it. But something blocks his way. So he has to risk more to get it. But something more difficult blocks the way again. So he risks still more and more to overcome more demanding obstacles. This scenario creates tension and conflict.

Structurally, the story of Jonah is very straightforward. But it remains a good example. Jonah wants to get away from God's command, so he takes a boat to go to another country. First obstacle? A storm. He waits the storm out below deck, hoping it is unrelated to him, hoping it'll go away. But it doesn't. Next obstacle? The captain pounds on his door, demanding that Jonah pray to his God for them. But Jonah refuses or ignores the demand. Next obstacle? Perhaps the captain drags Jonah to his quarters where the captain, the sailors, and the other passengers begin to draw lots to find the guilty party. Jonah watches the proceedings warily, wondering whether or not to gamble on the outcome. Ah, but there's a problem. If the lot falls to another sailor, he'll die for Jonah's disobedience. Should Jonah step forward and admit his guilt? Maybe so. Or maybe it doesn't matter because the lot falls to him anyway. And on the story goes, leading to Jonah's being thrown overboard.

The middle of your play must work the same way. Your character wants something but is thrown into circumstances that seem to prevent his getting it. Louis Catron uses "but," "whoops!" and "uh-oh" as expressions to help establish plot twists. Romeo wants to marry Juliet *but* she belongs to the feuding family. Romeo wants to be reunited with Juliet when—*whoops!*—he gets the message that she is dead and *doesn't* get the message that it's a trick. Juliet expects to awaken to find her beloved Romeo waiting for her when—*uh-oh*—she awakens to find him dead at her feet.

Middle Rules and Reversals

Make no mistake, this part of your play isn't easy. In fact, it's the toughest part to get through. Great beginnings can come surprisingly easy. Even the idea for a climactic and satisfying end may spring to mind more readily than expected. But getting your audience from that great beginning to the satisfying end requires all the thinking and discipline you can muster.

How?

Unquestionably, you (of all people) must know what your protagonist wants. There's nothing interesting about a story where the protagonist doesn't want anything or doesn't know what he wants or hasn't the strength of will to get what he wants.

Plot complications and twists must be worked out intelligently and plausibly. Every move, every line, every action must have motivation and must be part of the rising action—or it doesn't belong. Every entrance and exit must further your story and create a new course of action for your protagonist. Perhaps a character arrives who gives your protagonist a piece of information he didn't know. Or a situation emerges that allows your protagonist a personal insight that will determine what he does next. In any event, if it doesn't contribute to the rising action, it should get pitched.

Acts and scenes should always end with suspense—that next question or series of questions to be answered. Or that something that'll make the audience care about what'll happen next. A delivery boy arrives with Jonah's tickets for the boat trip, and Jonah confidently exits the stage with his suitcase, relieved to be getting away. "A cruise is just what I need to forget about being a prophet!" he says as he goes.

Another scene on the boat. Jonah's cabin. The captain pounds on the door. Their dramatic encounter, as Jonah refuses to pray, ends with the captain demanding that Jonah come with him to draw lots (or Jonah's being dragged out by the sailors).

Make scene and act endings count. If they end weakly or passively, your audience will lose interest. End on a twist, a turn, or a *reversal*.

A reversal was first acknowledged by Aristotle as that moment when everything suddenly goes the opposite for your protagonist than intended. Aristotle mentions *Oedipus* as an example. The messenger comes to cheer Oedipus and free him from his concerns about his mother, but by revealing who he is, he produces the opposite effect. That piece of information reverses the play's direction. A reversal also intensifies the feeling in your audience of "Oh no, what's going to happen next?" or "How in the world is he going to get out of this one?"

The story of Jonah has several reversals. Getting thrown overboard in the middle of a cataclysmic storm is certainly one of them. Being swallowed by a large fish is certainly another.

However, reversal alone isn't enough, according to Aristotle. Reversal must lead to *recognition*—a change from ignorance to knowledge. Jonah's dunking is an interesting reversal, but it is meaningless if it doesn't lead to something else. In this instance, it leads to being swallowed by a fish, which then leads to Jonah's acknowledgement that he is lost without God.

The Climax

Your play's middle exists to create rising action, which leads to the climax of your play (usually at the end of Act II in a three-act play). Some say the climax is the "highest point of action" in your play, some say it is an "irreversible turning point," some say it is *both* resulting in the answer to your major dramatic question (will your protagonist get what he's after?).

I'll compromise and say that the climax can be all of the above.

One reason is because the climaxes in the best plays appear to contain the highest point of action (or tension) as the protagonist's conflict reaches a point of no return. At that moment, the inciting incident, premise, goal, characters, rising action . . . everything seems complete.

But you mustn't confuse a play's climax with the traditional Hollywood climax, where the highest point of action is the shoot-out or car chase. In a play, the climax may well be the *least* exciting moment (in a sensational manner of speaking). The climax may be the quietest moment when the mother tells her daughter who her father really is. Or love is finally confessed between a man and a woman. Or a character dies.

However your climax is introduced, one rule is certain: you must never take the climax out of your protagonist's hands. Romeo kills Tybalt. Jack shows Miss Prism the handbag. Jonah tells the sailors to throw him overboard.

You will ruin your climax if your protagonist is acted upon, rather than taking action. It's a cheat that diminishes everything you've worked toward.

And at the risk of sounding heretical, it is unfair to use *deus ex machina* for your climax. *Deus ex machina* means literally "God from the machine"—a reference to Greek dramas when the climax involved lowering a large box onto the stage, whereupon an actor as a god would step out and solve all the problems. As Christians we may be tempted to take a similar tack by suddenly making our protagonist a Christian or having him or her receive an unexplainable spiritual gift or inspiration—like Batman conveniently pulling a ridiculous contraption from his utility belt—to resolve the situation. *Deus ex machina* can apply to any contrivance or artificially introduced element that'll change the direction or climax of your play.

Ah, but what about Jonah? Isn't that *deus ex machina*? I would argue that, in the context of Jonah's story, it isn't. We've established from the beginning that Jonah's story included—was even predicated on—his relationship with God. It was what motivated him to try to escape by boat. The storm (a major plot point) was God's doing. So it isn't inappropriate or unbelievable that Jonah would be swallowed and, in turn, saved by a large fish sent from God. God's involvement would've been inappropriate if He hadn't been known or referred to until Jonah was thrown overboard.

But I'll gladly accept letters arguing to the contrary, in care of this publisher. Just don't be surprised if I never answer.

The End

Your play's end contains the resolution, the denouement—the tying up of loose ends (not to create a happy ending, necessarily, but to satisfy any lingering questions in your audience's mind). If your middle is to play out the consequences of the beginning, then the end plays out the consequences of the climax. Order is restored. The audience's expectations are fulfilled. Satisfaction is attained. Or, in some cases, a final question is introduced—one clearly asked so that the audience will have something to think about as they leave the theatre (be warned, though: trying to be too pointed or clever about this may undo the satisfaction you've given your audience, and they'll leave the theatre thinking only about revoking your playwright's license).

Ideally, the denouement should be brief and should avoid surprise twists (except in a farce) or lengthy speeches that explain the meaning of the play. Respect your audience's intelligence. Leave well enough alone.

Beware of what is called an *anticlimax*. It's anything you add that undoes the overall effect of your play. For many, the story of Jonah is a good example of an anticlimactic ending. We've been through his experience of getting thrown overboard, he gets swallowed by a big fish, repents, preaches to Nineveh, *they* repent, and somehow one expects a satisfying ending that involves the entire town as they celebrate their newfound faith. As a "big finish" for a musical, it would be wonderful. But, no, the biblical chronicle doesn't end there. In the last chapter, we find Jonah sitting on a hillside pouting that he didn't get to see the destruction of the city. Big deal. As Scripture, it makes a valid point. As a story, it's an anticlimactic downer. In my work with the radio drama *Adventures in Odyssey*, I've adapted this story. You can be sure we had long discussions about whether or not to tell the full story *because* it's so anticlimactic. We did. And it was *only* in deference to God's Word. I wouldn't have bothered if it was any other work of literature.

Learn from Jonah.

EXERCISES

1. Write out your favorite *inciting incidents* from stories, plays, movies, or novels.

2. Write five of your own *inciting incidents* without worrying about plotting anything afterward.

3. Go back to questions from previous chapters about personal experiences and conflicts. Choose one and write out the climax. Now work backward from there to construct a plot that was *different* from your original experience.

4. Go back to your list of things that people want and how they get them. Now list the *obstacles* that get in the way of what people want.

5. In three sentences, plot the beginning, the middle, and the end of a play you've been working on.

6. Think of the climaxes to your favorite plays. What made them work so satisfactorily? How did the climaxes fulfill the major dramatic question? The protagonist's goal?

FIVE

Your Characters

What is a character? A factor whose virtues have not yet been discovered.
            —Lajos Egri, adapting a quote by Emerson[16]

Sanity in a writer is merely this: however stupid he may be in his private life, he never cheats in writing. He never forgets that his audience is, at least ideally, as noble, generous, and tolerant as he is himself (or more so), and never forgets that he is writing about people, so that to turn characters to cartoons, to treat his characters as innately inferior to himself, to forget their reasons for being as they are, to treat them as brutes, is bad art.
            —John Gardner[17]

Which comes first, the plot or the characters?

Please allow me to nip the question in the bud by saying very simply that I don't know. And neither do most writers and teachers and theorists. They may *think* they know, but most books show that, at best, they're equally divided on their answers.

For my money, I'll take the middle road and allow that, somehow, almost mystically, the two emerge together. As you think about a plot, certain characters will come to mind to help you fulfill that plot. As you think about specific characters, certain plot lines will come to mind that'll make the best use of those characters. Why not? Who says it *always* has to start one way all the time.

Plot and character coexist. A play that is all plot without a sense of character eliminates a fundamental interest for its audience: *humanity*. And yet, a play that spends two hours doing nothing more than studying a character without forward action and conflict eliminates another fundamental interest for its audience: *story*.

Inspiration

There are many places to go for inspiration about characters. You can think of people you know well or have met casually. You may remember people you've been told about. Ponder characters you've seen in movies or plays or read about in books. Look to the classics. Shakespeare, is one example. Charles Dickens is another. His books are filled with specific sorts of characters—all containing their own motivations, their own quirks and idiosyncracies. Then there's Victor Hugo, whose books make use of character *types*—individuals who represent more than their own desires to embody the desires of an entire section of the population. They're living symbols, not unlike some of the parabolic characters chronicled by Jesus. And we can't forget the comic characters who are larger than life, satirical, or absurd.

Which characters are most appropriate for your play?

That depends on your play, of course. As with all the other elements, your choice of character must be consistent with the tone you've created. They must fit within your play's reality, the universe that will engage your audience for an evening. For example, would it make sense to write a very serious play centered around a couple struggling to save their marriage, then have a Harpo Marx-type character race into the second act blowing bicycle horns while making faces at the audience? Or would it seem appropriate to write a rib-tickling farce about two Laurel and Hardy-type bachelors who suddenly fall in love with the same woman— only to discover that she is the mother of a little girl who gets crushed under the wheels of a train at the end of Act I?

Horrific to think about, isn't it?

Yet you have to make those kinds of choices. You have to decide what is appropriate in your world. You have to know who your characters are and what roles they are to play in the action to come.

How Do We Know the Character?

Let's look at it from the other way around. Remember in high school when you had to analyze all those plays and books in your literature class? Well, maybe not. But there were a few very basic guidelines to help us understand the characters.

Do you remember?

First, we know a character by what the character does—or doesn't do. Action can speak louder than words when an avowed coward suddenly rises to an occasion and behaves bravely. Or an avowed hero remains idle when bravery is needed. Within your play, what conflict have you created that will *show* what your characters are made of? What will you have them do—or *not do*?

Action, or the absence of it, is vital to how you communicate the character you've created.

Second, we know a character by what the character says. Unless your character really is Harpo Marx, your character will talk. What will he or she say? And what can we learn about the character when we read between the lines? Let's say your character is in a very intense encounter with his recently promoted boss—an undeserving man promoted into the position your character was supposed to get. His first act is to demote your character. The air is thick with tension between them. The argument starts, feelings are laid out. And suddenly your character begins to talk about the weather or the cracked paint on the office ceiling.

What does that tell us about your character?

When your character should speak, he is silent. What do we make of that?

Dialogue, or the absence of it, is vital to how you communicate the character you've created.

Third, we know a character by what the *other* characters say about him and how they treat him. They disrespect him, abuse him, possibly ignore him. They hang on his every word, laugh with him, treat him with kindness or sympathy. Your peripheral characters are *very* important in how your audience will understand a character.

Imagine a play where we've had several scenes involving two so-called friends. Yet one friend (call him Frank) keeps telling the other (named Ernest) that nobody likes him. In fact, they despise him. They only endure Ernest because they feel sorry for him. Ernest trusts his friend and is willing to believe him on this. Yet, later in the play, we see Ernest in an encounter with another character and get every impression that the other character genuinely likes him. Maybe Ernest doesn't see it—or thinks it's only an act of sympathy—but the audience forms an impression apart from what Ernest may think. That impression may be that Frank was lying for some reason. Or we may think that the other character really *is* motivated by sympathy, confirming Frank's statement and creating in our minds distinct feelings about Ernest and why he is despised.

So you can see how every word, every action is going to further your audience's perception of who your characters are and what they want.

So . . . Who Are They?

Your audience can know only as much as *you* know about your character. If you have just a vague notion of who your character is, that vagueness will show and will likely contribute to your audience's dissatisfaction with your play. Few of us can relate to an abstract notion. If you know your character inside and out—even more than you may ever reveal in your play—then your audience will respond to the richness of the humanity found within your character. Give your character a sense of history—a life that existed before he walked onstage and exists whenever he *isn't* onstage (unless you killed him, of course). Think about your character's background. Write it all out, if you can. A biography. Every detail that'll transform a one-dimensional idea—a stick figure on a page—into a living, breathing person with flesh and blood, wants and desires, experiences and dreams.

You *must* know as much about your character as you possibly can before you start your play. Granted, new ideas and innovations will emerge as you write. But get the basics down first. One way to establish them is to have your character fill out an exhaustive job application (and then some!). Full name (where did it come from? was he named after someone?), age, family relationships (wife? children?), sex, height and weight, color of hair, eyes and skin, overall appearance, work experience, education, political inclinations, extended family details (parents, brothers, sisters, family heritage, etc.), religion (current and upbringing), position in the community, hobbies, personal qualities and abilities, frustrations and failures . . .

Is your character an introvert or an extrovert? What is his philosophy of life? What kind of moral standards does he have? Does he have any psychological complexes—compulsive behavior, inhibitions, phobias? Any physical handicaps?

Consider these questions and more while remembering that the essence of being *human* is what you hope to achieve with the characters you create. This isn't a mortician's checklist you're filling out. This cadaver of facts and information has to get up and move. He must be fully human, a sensory and emotive being in time and space. He has to act and be acted upon. He must *want* something. He must engage in conflict to get it. What you know about him is the springboard of what you will have him say and do.

Yet it's important to remember not to confuse the reality of your character with *real people*. Just as drama is a heightened reality, your characters are heightened in their humanity. They can't just love, they must experience *great love*. They can't be insecure, they must be *paranoid* or *compulsive*. Your characters—like your plot—are under the magnifying glass you've created, showing how they behave in a very carefully structured situation.

Another consideration is what you want your audience to feel about your characters. Do you want your audience to like the character or not? Maybe sometimes but not always? Will they feel empathy? Sympathy? Apathy? Perhaps you want the audience to loathe him while understanding his motivation for being such a cad.

What do you want the audience to feel, and how will you achieve those feelings?

What about the *number* of characters in your play? That depends on what your play is about. You must have a protagonist in conflict with an antagonist, but secondary characters may bring much needed depth, comic relief, and texture to your play. Let's consider all three for a moment.

Your Protagonist

We've discussed your protagonists and antagonists elsewhere, but they're worth mentioning again in the context of character development.

Who is your protagonist? It's the character your play is about. It's the protagonist's central goal, wants, desires, and the ensuing conflict that gives the play its forward motion. Simplistically speaking, the protagonist is the good guy—the one your audience will care about and identify with and through whom your play will have meaning.

This doesn't mean your protagonist is always "good" or without flaws. As we've already established, your characters need to be multidimensional, thus your protagonist should have depth of humanity.

I won't get lost in a treatise about *antiheroes* made popular in plays and films over the last 30 years, but I have to point out the danger of basing an entire play on a character your audience will never like or relate to. Yes, wonderful points have been made in certain plays where this happened, but points don't often make for a satisfying or memorable evening in the theatre. I've seen and read plays where the lead character was completely unredeemable. I walked away wondering why I wasted my time and money.

Your Antagonist

Who is your antagonist? He or she is the main source of *conflict* for your protagonist (and since drama is conflict, you must have him or her). But your antagonist may not always be a he or a she. Your antagonist may be a group of hes and shes. Or your antagonist may be an it. Or it may be another side of the protagonist. Your antagonist is the force that opposes your protagonist's goal. In one way or another, your antagonist presents the obstacles, making it harder and harder for your protagonist to get what he or she wants.

For that reason, your antagonist must be equal to, perhaps even more powerful than, your protagonist. There's no real conflict if your antagonist isn't a formidable opponent. Naturally, the story of David and Goliath comes to mind. Goliath was a wonderful antagonist because he was huge, powerful, arrogant, and gave us deep satisfaction when he was brought down by the shepherd's stone.

As an antagonist, Goliath gave us something else—a means to test our protagonist. Through Goliath, we saw what David was really made of (and what Saul *wasn't* made of). A good antagonist actually brings out the best and worst aspects of your protagonist. Your protagonist has more dimension as a character because of your antagonist.

Allow me to mention again what I've said before: it's one of the great struggles in moralistic writing to keep your bad guy from being more interesting than your good guy. I've learned this particularly in writing for children and teens. The protagonists come off as good but ineffective wimps. The antagonists are charismatic and delightfully wicked. Yeah, they'll get their comeuppance by the end, but what a great time they'll have until then. Whereas your good guy may win, but he'll go on living a boring, wimpish life.

I'm sure there are many psychological theories for why children and many adults are drawn more to the bad guys than to the good guys. Frankly, I blame the writer. The antagonist is only as interesting as the playwright makes him. Or, as the animated Jessica Rabbit complained in *Who Framed Roger Rabbit?* "I'm not bad, I'm just drawn that way."

Your Secondary Characters

If you've been writing for a church, then it's no surprise that the number of characters you create may be determined by who's available. I once wrote a play called *Camp W* and can confess here and now that the number of characters wasn't based on artistic reasons but on the necessity of giving everyone in my youth group something to do. The same was true for *The First Church of Pete's Garage.* My plays originally written for the Jeremiah People—*Snapshots and Portraits, Family Outings,* and *Stop the Presses!*—had very specific character needs based on how many could afford to tour that year.

If you hope to get your play published or produced, it's helpful to consider two things. One, publishers are very sensitive to the number of characters in your play because it may affect sales. If most churches in the nation have small drama groups, plays with large casts may be a no-go. If most drama groups have more women than men, plays with more men than women could be a problem. If you're considering offering your play to professional theatrical producers, remember that every character costs them money. Budget—not quality—may determine whether your play gets seen or not.

However, we can't be like the emperor in *Amadeus* who griped that Mozart's music had "too many notes." How many secondary characters do you need? As many as are necessary. No more, no less. What do they add to the overall texture of your play? Do they help further the action, or are they distractions? Do they help to clarify the characters of your protagonist or antagonist? Or, as Catron asks, do they *"serve* the play"?

In some of my own work, I've found that secondary characters actually brought the play to life. Through them, I could challenge the protagonist or antagonist. As a friend of the protagonist, a secondary character makes a great foil or a fool—someone to ask aloud the questions the protagonist should be asking, or the audience may be wondering about. *"Why are you doing this? Are you nuts?"* the friend cries out and echoes the sentiments of the entire audience as the protagonist relentlessly pursues his or her goal. Secondary characters can bring a sweet voice of reason or conscience to a conflict out of control. Or they can become the unwitting hindrance, working for the antagonist to thwart the protagonist's plans.

Whoever they are or whatever they do in your play, make sure they *count.*

The Ring of Truth

You must've known I'd get back to this sooner or later. The ring of truth. Do your protagonist, antagonist, and secondary characters ring true to the time, place, setting, and style you've created? Are they *real* in your world, or do they seem like manipulated puppets at your mercy? Are their words and actions plausible to the situation you've thrust them into? Will your audience understand or empathize with the whys and wherefores of the characters in your play? Will your characters' experiences and behavior resonate with the audience's own experiences? Have you created characters who accurately represent humanity in its many forms? In other words . . . do they have the *ring of truth?*

EXERCISES

1. Where do you start to create a character? Write down one strong identifiable trait and build from there. (Your character is determined, naive, pure, weak, conceited, wise, abusive, etc.)

2. Consider the story of David and Bathsheba. Now write out biographies of each character involved. For each one, ask, Who am I and what do I want? What might be motivating each one in the actions taken? What was each one thinking and feeling as decisions were being made? Was David driven by blind lust? What was Bathsheba thinking when she came to David? Do you think Nathan was nervous as he approached the king with God's condemnation of his act?

3. Write out a list of words describing people in general (greedy, affectionate, ambitious, etc.). Now write a brief character description that embodies each word. Then write out what is in that character's background that made him or her become the word you picked.

4. If you're working on a play, give a thorough description (or biography) of your protagonist. Do the same for your antagonist. Now compare the two. How are they alike? In what ways are they different? Do they have similar goals? Why does your protagonist want what he or she wants? Why does your antagonist want to stop your protagonist? How can you sharpen their conflict?

5. Write two short "interviews" with your protagonist and then your antagonist, asking them directly the questions from Number 4 (and more).

6. List the most idiosyncratic people you know and what makes them that way.

7. Go back to your lists from Question 3 with one column of descriptive words and another column of character descriptions. Mix and match the words with the characters. (For example, what if you connect "greed" with a character who is painfully shy?) What kinds of characters do you come up with?

SIX

Dialogue

The dialogue of this author is often so evidently determined by the incident which produces it, and is pursued with so much ease and simplicity, that it seems scarcely to claim the merit of fiction, but to have been gleaned by diligent selection out of common conversation, and common occurrences.

—Samuel Johnson, in his *Preface to the Plays of William Shakespeare* (1765)

Dialogue is the words your characters say to each other. That's it in a nutshell, right?

Half right; thanks for playing.

Dialogue is more than just words; it's verbal action. It's a combination of words and silences that propel your play forward. It shows us who your characters are—or who they want others to *think* they are. It communicates in terms your audience can understand. It can be terse and gritty or beautifully poetic. It draws your audience in emotionally. It subtly articulates your theme and your personal beliefs. It has its own unique style—completely separate from words read on a page—because it is meant to be spoken out loud as a specific outlet for a specific character. It's also set apart from its sister form—screen dialogue—because movies are based on visual images while plays are dependent on words. When written correctly, it sounds real to your audience's ears, yet *isn't* real because it avoids real life's rambling, meaningless chit-chat that starts nowhere and ends nowhere. Dialogue is structured but must never sound like an organized speech because it comes spontaneously from your character's heart, filled with all the motivations contained there. Dialogue, as you can see, is many things. But one thing it must never be is boring.

Choosing Your Style

I remember showing an early draft of *Catacombs* to a friend. I had purposely attempted a style of dialogue that was pseudo-Shakespearean

—lofty, poetic. Somehow I thought it would articulate the feelings of the characters better. My friend laughed at me. He couldn't imagine why I'd write such clichéd and hokey-sounding garbage. Nobody talks like that. Why did I think these characters would? I didn't have an answer. "A neat idea," I may have mumbled as I walked away. But I knew he was right. I rewrote the play.

I'm not saying that lofty and poetic dialogue is wrong. In the case of *Catacombs*, it was simply inappropriate.

Where is your play taking place? In what time? The answers to those questions will determine the style of your dialogue.

If you know your characters as well as you should, then you know how they should talk. That also determines the style of your dialogue.

What genre are you writing within? A mystery? A raw urban thriller? A romantic comedy? Genre will determine the style of your dialogue.

Whatever you choose, your style must be *appropriate* to those choices.

Once More from the Heart

The marriage between dialogue and character cannot be overemphasized. Dialogue rings true when it seems as if it comes spontaneously from within your characters. It reflects their dreams, goals, aspirations, deceits, secret motivations, and emotions. You can put words in their mouths, sure, but your audience will know if it isn't true to who that character *is*.

A particularly satisfying moment in your experience as a playwright is when you suddenly realize that your characters aren't speaking for *you* anymore—they're speaking for themselves. And it's so true to who they are. No one else could say that line quite like that. The phrasing, the kinds of words used, the pauses, the incomplete sentences—they're all unique to that one character.

It reflects the character and, in many ways, *defines* the character. Your audience will have expectations for your character based on what your character says, as well as what he does. Or *bad* dialogue can neutralize expectations and kill whatever makes your character special.

A Maximum Offense

There's a particularly telling moment in an early Woody Allen film when one of his characters suddenly launches into a deep and meaningful monologue that seems completely inappropriate to who he is and what has been going on up until then. As he speaks, the words "Author's Message" begin flashing in one corner of the screen. Just in case we missed it.

How often have you seen a play or movie where a character seems to step outside of himself to talk about an important thematic idea? Too often, probably. And it's a perfect way to neutralize your characters and the credibility of your play.

Now, I won't say that Christians alone are bad about betraying their characters with preachy dialogue, but our zealousness in making sure our message is heard tends to make us prone to that problem.

We've talked about the dangers of "preaching" through drama elsewhere, but betraying your characters—making them say things they would not say in order to communicate *your* message—is doubly insulting to your audience.

An Ear for Dialogue

This is an often-used phrase for writers who can write effective dialogue. They've trained their ears and writing skills to translate realistic conversation, speech patterns, and qualities into dramatic dialogue. Neil Simon has a remarkable ear for dialogue, even though *no one* is as consistently funny in real life as his characters are. Try reading a David Mamet play with his machine-gun style of dialogue. He, like Harold Pinter, says a lot in very few words. An ear for dialogue can only be developed with a lot of time and attention spent listening to people, reading and watching plays and movies, and listening to actors read your lines out loud. The latter suggestion is especially helpful for weeding out sentences that "read well on the page" but don't speak well, awkward structure, poor word choices (words that don't sound right even when, technically, they're correct), disruptive rhythm patterns or repetitious word or rhythm patterns, and other problems you wouldn't catch when "hearing it in your head."

Verbal Action

Just as every physical activity must be motivated and further the action in your play, every *word* must be motivated and further the action. There has to be a reason your character is speaking, and that reason must take us forward in your plot.

Exposition in Dialogue

Exposition, like many other subjects we've discussed, has two schools of thought behind it. One is that exposition, by definition, "is exposing something." Thus, all plays contain exposition from start to finish because plays are constantly exposing the words and behavior of your characters. The other school limits exposition to background information verbalized by your characters. It's the talk that helps set up your play or presents key facts about your characters. For our purposes, let's stick to the latter definition.

Exposition is necessary to your play—it's unavoidable, since not *all* bits of information can be converted to behavior. Exposition is often found at the beginning of the play or of subsequent acts. But, as with all dialogue, the audience must never realize that you're purposely feeding them information. Exposition must be subtly buried in what your characters say and how they say it.

For example, if two characters tell each other things that they would obviously already know, then your audience will smell a rat. You're feeding them exposition.

If the action stops in order to provide information, your audience will realize that the playwright wasn't very adept at playwriting.

So what are the rules of thumb for dealing with exposition?

Oscar Wilde states that, "Action may always be interrupted by exposition when the latter is of the same or of a greater degree of interest."

In other words, don't interrupt your action for speeches and dialogue that take away from the forward movement of your play—*unless* the exposition can match the action you're interrupting.

On another, more practical note, Louis Catron suggests hiding exposition in the middle of sentences or speeches; avoid putting them in dominant positions like the beginning or end of a line.

Another technique: reveal your exposition in small chunks, preferably where the information will help propel the action forward. Use exposition to your best advantage so the discovery of that little tidbit of knowledge—whatever it may be—will motivate your characters. Exposition need not be a burden. In many cases, that piece of information could be the proverbial ace up your sleeve.

Exposition in Narration

Using a narrator in your play is another way to present background information. However, there are pitfalls with this once-popular convention. For one thing, a narrator can become a crutch for the playwright. Rather than think through clever, more appropriate ways to communicate exposition, the playwright simply takes the easy way out and hands the task over to a narrator. There are exceptions, of course, but it's best to have a narrator as a *last* resort—not as a first choice.

Dialogue Techniques

While the following techniques can become overused and clichéd, used carefully, they can be effective forms of dialogue (sometimes without words) to communicate emotion.

Ellipsis

"I wonder if . . . no, probably not. I mean, why would she . . . no, never mind."

The ellipsis is one way to break up a sentence in order to show a character's frame of mind—nervous, distracted, unsure, confused, or just wound-up in general.

Interruptions

"Just what do you think you're—"
"Get back or I'll shoot."

Interruptions can be a terrific tool for capturing hard-edged emotion. The staccato, rapid-fire effect heightens tension between characters and strengthens conflict. In other cases, it may position one character as stronger than another.

"Look, I was just trying to say—"
"Pass me that milk, will ya?"
"Right. Anyway, I want you to know—"
"I wonder what's on the television tonight?"

Half-finished sentences

"I've been thinking a lot [about it] . . . Was there something I should've said that would, you know . . . [make it clearer]?"
"No . . . [not at all]. I understood exactly what you . . . [meant]."

The brackets finish the sentence, but the lines themselves allow for the character to drift off, shrug, make a face or gesture to imply the end of the line. I've used this technique for characters who are distracted, inarticulate at a time of stress, or simply dependent on physical gestures (as many people are) to convey what they're feeling.

Replace words with physical action

As in the previous example, words can be discarded in favor of very natural physical gestures. Though, it may be more precise:

"Are you going to—(gestures to the door impatiently) or what?"

Physical action may also serve as an entire line. For example, in response to something your character has just said, your other character may express more by throwing a balled-up piece of paper into the trash can than by articulating a line that expresses his feelings.

I'm not aware of any standard uses of dots and dashes, though dashes are best known for cutting off a line or a thought while dots seem to imply a continuation of some sort.

Just for fun, here's part of a sketch written for Jim Custer and Bob Hoose in *Fathers Anonymous*. It incorporates some of the techniques just mentioned to create a particular effect.

The Big Game

(MAX enters. He is juggling a bowl of potato chips, bags of pretzels and more cans of soda than one person can handle. It's a Super Bowl kind of occasion, and MAX is geared up. He looks around and realizes he doesn't have enough chairs (in fact, there aren't any). He growls and, still balancing the food and drinks, goes offstage only to return a moment later with the food, the drinks *and* a couple of folding chairs. What follows is an amazing feat of balance as MAX tries to unfold the chairs and set them up without putting down the food and drinks. At it's most comical, BRAD—still dressed in a suit from work—arrives and rescues him.)

BRAD: What in the world are you—?

MAX: You're late.

(BRAD helps MAX get set up as they talk, though BRAD's enthusiasm isn't as great as MAX's.)

BRAD: Work. Y'know.

MAX: Kickoff—what? Two minutes? (Turns on TV)

BRAD: Hey— (Spreads his arms as if to say, "I know and I'm sorry I'm late but I got stuck at the office") OK?

MAX: Big game. Really big game.

BRAD (pulls at his tie, takes off coat): I'm here.

MAX (nods and gestures to TV, as if to say, "I've been waiting all day for this"): Man!

BRAD: Yeah. Judy?

MAX: No way. Out. I said, "Big game. You take the kids and—gone." Can't have a lot of y'know when I'm trying to watch (gestures to TV, cups hands as if passing a ball).

BRAD: I didn't even go home first. Laura would've had me goin' and y'know not watching and—

MAX: They don't get it. I try to say, "Hey, here's why it's so you know" and she just—(Shakes his head as if to say, "She doesn't understand") Have a pretzel. (Suddenly shouts at TV) Let's go! Do it!

BRAD (takes a pretzel, but there's something bothering him): Yeah!

MAX: I need this. I don't wanna get all, you know, philosophy and stuff, but there are times. There are really times.

BRAD: I know.

MAX: It's like you wanna get right down there on the field and—man. Win. Gotta win.

BRAD: I know.

MAX: That's what it's all about. The game, right? It's life. Forget all that y'know—fair play, sportsmanship—you gotta do what it takes. You gotta, you know, be good. You gotta win.

BRAD (thoughtfully): Win.

MAX (looks at BRAD): What?

BRAD (raises his drink as if in a toast): Win.

MAX (responding in kind): Win! That's right. Success, you know?

BRAD: Yeah, success.

MAX: My old man knew. He drilled it—(gestures to his brain) day in, day out.

BRAD: Mine too.

I'll be the first to admit that *what's* being said in this sketch has been said many times before by other writers. *How* it's being said has made this sketch extremely popular with Custer and Hoose's audiences.

Beats and Pauses

A *beat* in a line is an intentional break in the rhythm to establish a new rhythm. For example, a *beat* might be used to show an abrupt change of thought on the part of your character.

"It just occurred to me that—(Beat) Hey, wait a minute. What did you just say?"

       or

"I promised myself I'd never do that again. (Beat) When did you say the train is coming?"

A *pause* is also an intentional break in the line or rhythm but not always to change the rhythm or accomplish a change of thought. Sometimes it *furthers* the character's thought.

"It just occurred to me that . . . (pause) I'm not really sure of myself. I'm afraid of what's going to happen."

       or

"I promised myself I'd never do that again. (Pause) It was so horrible the first time . . . I can't stand to think about it."

Both beats and pauses can also come in between character's lines.

Sentence Structure

The strongest positions in a sentence are at the beginning and the end. The same is true with speeches. If you have an important idea or piece of information to communicate, don't bury it in the middle.

Names are a good example of this. Which is stronger?

"I don't understand what you're talking about, Jeff."

       or

"Jeff, I don't understand what you're talking about."

I hope you picked the second one. Using a name at the start of the line demands attention, not only from the character being spoken to but also from your audience. (But don't use proper names too often. Not only does it sound unnatural, but also it diminishes the potency when you *do* use names.)

The beginnings and ends of sentences and speeches are also the bridges from one line or speech to another. It's the moment when both relay racers are touching the baton, handing from one to the other until the baton is carried to the next racer. And, like the relay race, your dialogue should move us smoothly and gracefully from the beginning to the end.

Pitfalls and Common Mistakes

Let's round off our discussion of dialogue with some of the pitfalls and mistakes *any* playwright can make.

Show, don't tell. This is a "golden rule" of any good writing. I can simply have my character tell you he's angry, or I can have him throw a cup against the wall and scream for everyone to leave him alone. Which do you think will have the biggest impact on your audience? Use action, words with strong images to *show* your audience what's happening rather than *telling* them.

Avoid long, complex sentences. Not only can they be mind-numbingly boring, but they can dilute the power of what your character is saying. Keep lines short and concise. Your actors will love you for it.

Avoid incorporating more than one idea or emotion in speeches. Long, complex sentences and speeches that try to convey more than one emotion or idea will come off convoluted and confused. Your audience can only track with so much at a time.

Don't let characters articulate emotions too easily . . . use unfinished sentences, etc. Characters who are too articulate sound insincere, as if the emotion has come to them too easily. In my experience people are *less* articulate when caught up in strong emotions. In dialogue, this is where you'll want to use unfinished sentences, interruptions, and ellipsis to help communicate your character's inner emotional turmoil.

Clichés. Clichés speak for themselves. It's all too easy to the let the cat out of the bag if your character has a chip on his shoulder and has to resort to clichés to say what's on his mind. Know what I mean?

And we have to consider *Christian* clichés too. Jesus is the answer because He wants you to have an abundant life, true, but Christianity isn't just a religion, it's a way of life.

The worst combination can be found in so-called evangelistic plays where a Christian gets into a debate with a character who isn't a Christian and, of course, the Christian always gets the verbal upper-hand with clever responses and cute retorts.

Nobody wins with that kind of dialogue.

Verbal bell-bottoms. Here I'm talking about clichés, phrases, colloquialisms, and popular expressions that are timely when you write your play but only date your work when spoken five years later. "See you later, alligator." "Groovy!" "Right on!" "Have a good one." "Radical!" Unless you're trying on purpose to capture a time period, I strongly suggest avoiding any and all time-dated references so your work will have longevity.

Minimize parenthetical directions. For the most part, don't burden your play with a lot of parenthetical directions—either with character emotion or stage directions. With the former, you shouldn't need to spell out how your character is feeling. The context and line should do the job for you. Likewise for the latter, you don't want to lock the actors or the director or set designer into precise blocking by spelling everything out. When it comes to parentheticals, say only what is absolutely necessary.

Dialect, idiom, and unique patterns of speech. Unless you're really, really good at capturing these slippery critters, don't put them in your script. The result could be embarrassing for you, your actors, and your audience. I am a white protestant male, and I won't pretend to know the precise ways that an inner-city black (African-American?) woman may speak—or an Italian or a New York Jew or an inestimable number of other ethnic groups. That won't stop me from writing such characters into a play, or researching general phrases or idioms to get the right flavor, but I'd rather let a competent director and actor translate my lines *into* the character than write them all out like Mark Twain did in *Huckleberry Finn*.

EXERCISES

1. In a previous chapter, I suggested that you "interview" your characters. Thinking more carefully about the importance of dialogue, go back and interview them again with an ear toward *how* they answer your questions.

2. Take the following expositional facts and turn them into a short scene between two characters who are old friends who happen to meet at a bus stop after being apart for several months. Bury the exposition.

   *The spouse of one of the characters has just died. The other knows it, but has not expressed condolences.

   *One of the characters is bitterly angry at the other character for not attending a surprise birthday party.

   *One of the characters recently lost a job, the other got a promotion.

   *Both characters went to the same high school together and loved the same woman (or man, as the case may be).

3. Try writing the scene from Question 2 in several styles: with poetic dialogue, terse dialogue, dialogue with a lot of fragmented sentences, and dialogue that consists mostly of physical action to complete sentences.

4. Write a sketch in which two Christian characters speak *only* in Christian clichés.

5. Write from memory a conversation you had or heard today. Now rewrite that conversation as a fictional dramatic scene, paying close attention to the elements we have discussed in this chapter.

SEVEN

Evaluating Your Play

Just when that first draft is finished and you think it's over . . .

It's not.

The time has come to *revise*.

Revision is what separates stageworthy plays from plays that sit in your filing cabinet. Revision is what separates good playwrights from mediocre ones. All the best-known writers do it—Neil Simon, Tennessee Williams, Arthur Miller, Eugene O'Neill—not only *before* their plays make it to production, but during and after too. The script is sacred, but only for a moment. It demands your constant attention.

Yes, there's a point when you have to let go. But that point can only come when you're truly satisfied that it's the best it can ever be. Fortunately and unfortunately, many of my plays were published not long after the initial performance. I say "unfortunately" because the play was locked up in print; the revisions my later sensibilities knew the play needed couldn't be included. So I cringe every now and again when I stumble across one of the published plays.

What are good ways to evaluate your work?

Put It Aside

Once you've finished a first draft, put it aside for a day or so (maybe longer). Detach yourself from the work you've done, giving room between what you *hoped* to accomplish and what you actually *did* accomplish. Then pick the manuscript up and look at it again more critically (by critically, I don't mean thrashing yourself with feelings that you're an awful writer or you had no business trying to write such a project in the first place, I mean *constructive* criticism).

Read It Out Loud

A play is supposed to be performed. Listen to how it sounds—for the overall effect. Don't change anything at first, simply make notes. In general, does the play *do* what you want it to do? Will the audience feel what you want them to feel? Is the plot plausible? Do your characters' motivations make sense?

Read the play out loud a second time, paying closer attention to the dialogue. Do the sentences say what you meant them to say? Are there unintentional word repetitions? Does a speech go too long? Is the dialogue true to your characters? Again, don't make the changes right then. Make notes for your revision later.

Pizza Night

Put your fragile ego on the shelf, invite trusted friends or actors over, feed them pizza, and let *them* read your play *out loud*. A cold, objective reading from those who don't know what you were trying to do with your play can be enlightening.

Afterward, it may be helpful to ask your friends what they thought of the play. What did they think of the characters, the dialogue, the characters' motivations, and the conflict? Any inconsistencies? What were their overall impressions of what the play was about? Was it satisfying for them? Were there things that didn't make sense? Were there scenes or lines that went too long? Take copious notes—not as dictations of what you'll *have to* change but as *possible* changes to consider later.

Local theatre groups or workshops may be willing to read your play for you as well.

Ask Yourself the Hard Questions

Because if you don't, somebody else will. Probably a critic.

- Does your play ultimately say what you wanted it to say? Does it achieve your goals and fulfill your intentions?

- Is every aspect, twist, or turn in your plot plausible and intelligent? Is it comprehensible to your audience?

- Do you have a clear beginning (inciting incident), middle (rising action), and end (climax and resolution)?

- Will your audience *care* what will happen next? Are your scenes compelling, guiding the audience from one step to the next?

- Is your conflict clearly understood? Do all aspects of your play contribute to the forward movement of the conflict?

- Are you, the author, ever exposed—caught operating behind the scenes and between the lines of your play?

- Are your characters defined? Is your protagonist and his or her goals clear? Is your antagonist of equal or greater strength to your protagonist? Do your obstacles and reversals make sense? Are your secondary characters necessary to your protagonist, antagonist, and the forward movement of the play?

- Do you *show* action or spend too much time *telling* what's going on?

- Is your dialogue natural and true to your characters? Can any lines be cut without hurting the play? Can multiple words be replaced with one word or action? Are there any long, unnecessary speeches? Are there any words used that are not commonly used in everyday language?

- Are lines, actions, entrances, and exits clearly justified by your characters' motivations?

- Does your climax bring to a head your major dramatic question? Does your play end with appropriate resolution for your plot and characters—or does it just seem to stop?

- Is the last moment of the play a satisfying experience for your audience?

- Consider your audience: will the play offend some of them? Why? Is that offense worthwhile in the context of your play?

Don't Despair

As I said, the best playwrights revise and revise and revise again. It's not uncommon to do 5 (and sometimes more than 10) drafts of a play before it's ready to be seen by an audience. And even then, their reactions will help you make still more revisions. As a craftsperson, you should expect it and, pain in the neck though it is, appreciate the insight revisions will give you for future plays.

EIGHT

Script Formatting

There are several script formats you can use for your play. Ideally, you should find out from prospective publishers which format they prefer. You may also want to take a look at the many published plays available at your local bookstore. In lieu of a publisher's specific direction, here are a few basic formats for you to try.

The Start

In all cases, your play should have a title page. The title, subtitle, and type of play (one-act, three-acts, etc.) should be centered on the page. Under that, your name. At the bottom you may want to note your copyright ownership: © 1995, Your name. Always include on the title page your full address and phone number.

On the next page, again put the title centered at the top, with your name centered beneath it. Beneath that, indicate cast of characters with their specific names and brief description of who they are. Beneath the cast, put the *time* in which your play is set. Beneath that, a description of the *place* where your play is set, followed by each act and scene and the place where they are set. Or:

JONAH

by B. G. Whaler

Cast of Characters

JONAH: *A middle-aged prophet; on the run from God.*

CAPTAIN AHAB: *A cantankerous sea captain; on the run from a storm.*

SEAMAN GLIB: *The first mate.*

The Time

Sometime in the Old Testament (450 B.C.?)

The Place

Act One.   Scene One. Jonah's apartment. Night.
            Scene Two. The Travel Agency. The next morning.

Act Two.   Scene One. The S.S. Cursed. The next morning.
            Scene Two. The S.S. Cursed. That afternoon.

Act Three. Scene One. The Belly of a Whale. That evening.
            Scene Two. Nineveh. Three days later.

The first page of the play should have the title again with Act One and Scene One centered beneath it. Below that, a more detailed setting description can be given—so the reader will have a description of the set as seen when the curtain rises. If it's Jonah's apartment, then describe the pertinent information about Jonah's apartment as a guide to future directors, set designers, and publishers.

Next, you'll describe the action as the curtain rises. And the play begins.

A More Traditional Format

Up to the rising of the curtain, the format mentioned above is pretty standard for most plays. Precisely how names, lines of dialogue, and stage directions appear on the page vary, depending on the playwright or the publisher. Here's the most traditional:

NAME OF CHARACTER IN CAPITAL LETTERS (parenthetical note):
    Followed by the line of dialogue, indented for as long as the line or speech continues.

(Double-spaced away from lines of dialogue, put any stage directions in parentheses, clearly stating who is supposed to be doing what and where. They may or may not be capitalized.)

Confused? Here's a chunk of a play called *Dear Diary* for your consideration.

SCENE ONE

(BILLIE enters and speaks to us as if we are her diary.)

BILLIE: Dear Diary . . . I had the strangest dream last night. It was kinda like one of those musicals, you know? People singing and dancing all over the place. Really weird. But, for a little while, I felt really happy. Like life was a lot of fun and Mom and Dad got along and I even liked Katie and didn't resent her for being so perfect all the time and . . . well, it was only a dream. Mom woke me up for school and everything was normal. (Beat) What a dream, though. (Beat) I gotta lay off having cold pizza before I go to bed.

(BILLIE enters the scene. The kitchen. A table sits with modest adornments. It is set for breakfast. A bowl of oatmeal sits with a spoon sticking straight up out of the top. Billie's MOTHER—Anne—moves across the stage, calling.)

MOTHER: Billie! *Billie!*

BILLIE (offstage): *Coming,* Mom!

MOTHER: You're going to be late for school *again,* and I'm *not* writing you another note. (Beat) That girl. (Beat, yelling) Your oatmeal's getting cold!

BILLIE: I'm coming!

(Billie's FATHER—David—enters, ready for work (blue collar). As he speaks, he takes his usual place at the table and retreats behind the paper—sports section, to be precise.)

FATHER: Yelling. Always yelling. A quiet morning—just once.

MOTHER (serving him a plate of something and coffee): A quiet morning? *You* play alarm clock for Billie and see if you can do it quietly. (Yelling) Billie!

BILLIE (entering): All right, all right. (Sits down at her usual place) Hi, Dad.

FATHER: The Bucks lost again.

BILLIE: Fine, thank you.

MOTHER: Did you clean your room? If I have to go in your room with it looking like it did last night, you'll be on restriction for a week. Understand?

BILLIE: Mom, I'm already on restriction.

MOTHER: Another week, then.

BILLIE: Mom, you've already got me on restriction for at least three weeks beyond a normal life span. What're you gonna do—exhume my body and make it stand in the corner? ·

(As the conversation continues, BILLIE is distracted, picks up the spoon still in the oatmeal. The whole bowl comes with it.)

MOTHER: Don't be smart. David.

FATHER (turning page, speaking automatically): You heard your mother, Billie.

MOTHER: Not that. Will you put the paper down and eat your breakfast?

FATHER: It's cold. Zap it for me.

MOTHER (growls): It wasn't cold when you sat down.

(MOTHER exits with FATHER's plate.)

BILLIE (seeing her opportunity, moves to her FATHER, shoving a pen and paper at him): Dad, you have to sign my report card. It's due back today.

FATHER (behind paper): Huh?

BILLIE (puts pen in his hand): Just sign.

And on it goes. With slight alterations, this seems to be a popular format for most of the published plays I've seen. But there's another, less common format . . .

Variations on a Screenplay

One format takes a pseudoscreenwriting approach to plays:

CHARACTER'S NAME HERE IN CAPITAL LETTERS
(Indented parenthetical instruction here.)
And the line itself goes here.

> CHARACTER'S NAME with
> specific stage direction goes here.

I haven't seen this format in very many places. But, for some, it may be the cutting edge of what's to come.

NINE

Assorted Business, Commissioned Works, and What to Do with Those Perplexing Songs

Since agents for playwrights in the Christian market aren't in abundance, I thought it might be helpful to discuss a few business considerations.

First and foremost: never sign *anything* without getting advice from someone who knows the law. Also first and foremost: never sign *anything* that would have you relinquish your rights to the work you created for a one-time fee. You may be thrilled to have a producer or publisher want your work, but don't let that moment's thrill cause you to sign something you'll regret for a lifetime. Sometimes it's better to wait. Your church probably has a member who knows law or an accountant who can refer you to someone who knows. Ask around. Or check the yellow pages for a lawyer who might consult inexpensively about your contract. Better to pay a few dollars now for some help than make a mistake that'll cost you more dollars later.

Commissioned Works

As more and more churches look for unique ways to present the Christmas or Easter story, more and more writers are being asked to help out. I'm encouraged for two reasons. First, it means that churches are thinking more creatively than ever before. Second, it means that writers around the country will get a chance to sharpen their skills in new and exciting ways.

If you've been asked by a church to write a play or program, you may be feeling the exact opposite.

Why? Because they asked you to write an original Christmas story that *must* incorporate the entire Nativity story, plus the pastor's two sons, the church's *very popular* quartet, and the entire choir shaped like a Christmas tree.

It happens.

But maybe we should back up to the moment when you were first asked to do the writing. I can't say it enough. Get business out of the way first. Make absolutely sure everyone understands up front who ultimately *owns* what you're writing. Is it yours to offer to other churches or to try to get published—or does the church think it'll be theirs? How much do you expect to get paid (with additional payment for rewrites that aren't your fault: one of the pastor's sons came down with the flu and they want you to make it the music director's *daughter,* or the *very popular* quartet booked to perform at another church)? What is your deadline to deliver the script? Will there be music? Will you be expected to write the scenes as a segue in and out of the music?

Get the details—and a written letter confirming your understanding of your responsibilities—before you write a word on the play. It'll save you a lot of aggravation and sweat later.

The Request: Sketches and Songs

If your "client" (maybe the minister of music at the church) wants a series of sketches to link the latest and most popular seasonal songs together, then you'll have to think carefully about the order of the songs and how they build emotionally. In a sense, you're constructing a "play" without a dramatic backbone. Each scene must have it's own tone and emotion with readily identifiable characters (you won't have a lot of time for character development) that will hand off to the song. Like a revue, each sketch and song must guide the audience to a "climax" of emotion.

It's difficult to be specific, since your assignment will depend on the songs chosen. What do the songs say? What are their moods? If you were working on a Broadway musical, what kind of sketch would lead up to such a song? What kind of sketch should follow it?

I believe most "clients" would be grateful to hear you ask such questions and will happily work with you to construct an emotionally satisfying presentation.

The Request: Scenes and Songs

I'm giving *scenes* a decidedly different spin than *sketches.* By *scenes,* I'm referring to a program more like a play in that it has consistent characters who, scene by scene, tell a story. Maybe it's Mary and Joseph making their way to Bethlehem. Maybe it's a particular family who is trying to find the meaning of Christmas amid the hustle and bustle of the season. Your job as a playwright may be to write scenes (interspersed with music) that rise in action (as a play should) and get the audience to a climax that fulfills not only the needs of the characters but the musical expectations as well. No, really. I'm not kidding.

Again, I believe the Broadway musical-style is your best guide here. Outline the basic "story" you've worked out with your "client." Then listen to the songs, get to the heart of what they're about, assess their mood, and then work closely with your "client" about their best placement.

There are no hard-and-fast rules except to remember that you're the hired hand who must bring forward all your best knowledge and creativity to make their program work.

TEN

Writing, Reality, and Pet Peeves

The act of writing is a personal act. Ask every writer you know *how* he or she writes, and each one will have a different answer. I've written some plays in long-hand (yes, even *after* I'd owned a computer for several years). This book has been written with a laptop while I sat on my family room sofa, with my more formidable computer at my desk by the window, and on the same laptop in a cottage in the south of England. (Yeah, I know. It's tacky to invoke the image of a cottage in a foreign country. But I wanted you to be impressed.)

I've written in libraries, in offices, during church services, in restaurants, on planes, in trains, in automobiles, and hanging upside-down from the Washington Monument by shoelaces. Just kidding on that last one. The point is: the hack writer in me doesn't demand a particular locale for my writing.

That isn't true for everyone. Stop for a moment and think about where—and under what circumstances—you do your best writing. Maybe it's the kitchen table with a hot cup of coffee as the sun streams picturesquely through the window above the sink. Maybe it's that corner in the basement, far away from the rest of the house. Maybe it's right in the middle of a family room full of kids with the stereo on.

Wherever you choose to write, consider the following questions. Is it comfortable? Can you maintain a good writing posture to eliminate neck, back, and elbow pain (particularly with word processors)? Is it free of counterproductive distractions? Do you have within arm's reach the equipment you need—pens, pencils, paper, a word processor, a good dictionary, a thesaurus? Is it aesthetically pleasing to you? Can you get there easily and often? If the answer to any of these questions is no, you may want to rethink where you write.

Ah, but what if you find the perfect spot but still don't *feel* like writing? Write anyway. Better to waste a few hours writing something you may never use (unlikely since we writers are notorious recyclers) than wasting a few hours staring at a blank piece of paper.

I'll confess a few personal idiosyncrasies. Sometimes when I want to write but haven't quite gotten in the mood I'll allow myself an hour browsing in a favorite bookstore. For me, looking through books (of all sorts) reminds me that I love writing—and that I *am* a writer. Often I'll discover new inspiration, a new angle, a different perspective.

Unfortunately, I also discover the temptation to spend money I don't have on books I don't really need.

Distraction for a writer can be both healthy and unhealthy. It's a running joke in my house that when I'm about to do some serious writing I rearrange things. The books on the shelf, the compact discs, the furniture. I have a theory that I compulsively rearrange in order to work out the details of whatever project I'm about to write. It's an exercise to get my mind in order. Distractions can be unhealthy when they get in the way of writing. You go through the mail, you take another walk, you nibble mindlessly on food that isn't good for you, you flip channels on the TV . . . you'll do *anything* but write.

The first thing is to realize you're distracted. Don't justify it. Don't rationalize it. Call it for what it is. Then resist the temptation, difficult as that may be.

I know of some writers who operate on a reward system. They won't touch the day's mail or eat that snack or watch that movie unless they have finished a set amount of writing: a scene, 1,000 words, whatever. Try it for yourself to see if it helps.

Creative Insanity

It's little wonder writers go insane. Writing is a very solitary act that defies time and space; where a scene lasting one minute might take eight hours to write. Or 10 years may pass in three lines. Or you may spend hours thinking and rethinking a scene, playing it out to a proper conclusion over and over while the world outside spins past at its normal pace. In a day, whole nations have fallen while your character barely made it to the opposite side of the stage.

It's this aspect of writing that C. S. Lewis used to illustrate how God can take care of each one of us so thoroughly. Inasmuch as God is outside time, Lewis noted, He can spend as much time with us as an author can spend with each one of his or her characters.

The Passion and the Discipline

I've heard it said that a novelist must be prepared to spend at least a year immersed in his novel. I'd guess that a playwright needs no less time to write the first draft of a play. And then you have to figure in the time for subsequent drafts and revisions if a producer or director asks for them, not forgetting the various revisions you'll want to do *after* you've seen your play performed.

What makes it possible?

The *passion* you have for your subject. And the *discipline* to get the writing done. When one wanes, the other often kicks in. That's why I wrote at the beginning that it's best to choose premises that you truly believe in. If you don't think that what you're doing is worthwhile, then you'll have nothing to carry you to the end.

Know the Rules Before You Try to Break Them

This is an old expression. It's annoying in a way because it's such a cliché, yet it's so true. John Gardner wrote that "no ignoramus—no writer who has kept himself innocent of education—has ever produced great art."[18]

In my younger, more heady days, I didn't want to know what other playwrights had written. I wanted to keep my ideas "pure and original." I didn't want to be shackled by the rules other people followed to write their plays. I turned ignorance into a matter of pride.

Ultimately, such arrogance creates a creative well that easily runs dry. The inner springs can't maintain it, and the coverings of so-called originality keep all the fresh rain out. Personal experience becomes a rusty bucket.

Know and understand the rules before you dismiss them out of hand. They exist for a reason. To guide. To give you the benefit of the centuries of experience that led to this point in history. They don't have to be a constraint, but the tracks upon which your train can speed along.

Good grief. Dried up wells and choo-choo trains. Any other metaphors I can beat to death?

If you want to be a good writer, then *read*. If you want to be a good playwright, then *read* and *go to plays*. Study your craft. Know it. Be an expert—not as an academic exercise—but as a means to infuse your writing with the richness of all that has come before you. Solomon wisely said that there is nothing new under the sun. He wasn't kidding. So why pretend you're the only one who has ever written a play about unrequited love? Look at how the very best writers handled it, then filter it through your own style.

In other words, you can't be innovative unless you have the elements in hand with which to be innovative.

I confess. The inspiration for *Family Outings* came from reading Dr. James Dobson's *Love Must Be Tough.* Some of the sketches found in *Vantage Points* and other collections came from a play called *The Pearly Gates,* which was directly inspired by A. R. Gurney's *The Dining Room. Stop the Presses!* was inspired by *The Front Page* by Ben Hecht and Charles MacArthur. *A Work in Progress* and *Fathers Anonymous* was inspired by *Latins Anonymous,* an ensemble-based sketch revue I saw in San Diego. *Catacombs* was indirectly inspired by *The Mortal Storm* by Phyllis Bottome. I could go on, but you get the idea. My vanity would like to believe that what I write is original. But I know better.

Perception vs. Reality

As a writer, you are involved in the creation of entire worlds. From the point when the lights go up all the way to the final curtain, you've created a world that must engage your audiences. I've mentioned elsewhere that drama isn't reality but a *perceived* reality. It integrates the rules of real living with the rules you've created. For example, if you've written a realistic drama set in an office about a ruthless businessman who finds himself to be the worst victim of his own selfishness, your audience will be very surprised if your created world suddenly dispenses with the laws of gravity. What would it do to your play—your premise, your theme—if your characters floated on and off the stage, climbed the walls, and had to sit on desks to keep them from flying out the window? In other words, establish your reality and stick to it.

Even reality may betray our perceived reality, much like the sound of a gun discharging is a disappointing *pop* compared to the enhanced sound-effect gunfire used on television and in the movies. Because of this, I had to go through unbelievable gymnastics to get the gunfire at the end of a production of *Catacombs* to sound "right" to our audiences' ears. The starter pistol we used couldn't have been more authentic, but it didn't sound "right." Finally, we had to shoot it into a large metal trash barrel to get the depth and resonance so our audience would believe a gun was really being shot. We had to alter reality to match people's *perceived* reality.

In *Adventures in the Screen Trade,* William Goldman chronicles a completely implausible story about a man who breaks into a castle to see a very rich and powerful woman. The story is filled with convenient moments when a maid unlocks a window while our hero stands on the drainpipe outside, guards just happen to walk away as our hero approaches, he doesn't know the layout of the castle yet finds the woman's room, enters it because her normal guard happened to be taking the dogs out for a walk, and then finds himself face-to-face with the woman, who frantically buzzes for help on a sophisticated alarm system but isn't heard because *that* guard was off doing something else. Implausible, convenient, unbelievable.

Yet the story is completely true.

A gentleman named Michael Fagin sneaked in to see the Queen of England under more preposterous circumstances than that.

Goldman's point is that your audiences' *perceived reality* would never accept such a story on the stage or in a movie. They just wouldn't believe it.

A Guide and Manipulator

I once told a gathering of writers that the essence of writing was to manipulate the reader (or the audience) without getting caught. I was taken to task for using a negative word like *manipulate* in the same breath as writing. So I changed it to "guide." The writer must *guide* his or her readers (or audience) without getting caught.

In my mind, it still amounts to the same thing.

Your plot, characters, and dialogue must never seem contrived. What do we mean by contrived? It means they must never betray that you're a writer who is making them do and say the things they're doing and saying.

Think back to some of the worst moments you can remember in plays. Often they're the moments when you saw through the plot, characters, or dialogue to the writer beyond. And, at that moment, the plot became just a story and the characters were just actors saying lines. Your eye went from the puppets up the strings to the puppeteer. The illusion was blown.

As a writer, you must become invisible. You're the unseen force whose existence may be challenged by the characters you've created. But you're always there. You always know what's going to happen. You're in complete control even if no one on the stage or in the audience ever guesses or admits that you are.

Hm. Sounds a lot like someone else we all know, doesn't it?

Communicating Without Credibility

It's easy to complain about the people who won't take our writing seriously. The leadership at the church. Friends who simply can't understand why we're driven to write. Maybe even our spouses and children.

In a larger realm, we may complain about how society at large won't take us seriously.

I've been wondering why that seems to be true. In a nutshell, I think it has to do with credibility.

Imagine how you would feel if someone you hardly knew and certainly didn't know well enough to trust suddenly came into your house and started telling you how to clean it, make dinner, treat your spouse, or discipline your children. You may rightfully say, "You don't know anything about me! You don't know anything about my family or my house! How dare you come in here and presume to tell me what to do!" And you'd throw them out on their ears.

Imagine the same scenario at the office. Someone you don't know, without any background in your line of work, walks in and starts telling you how to do your job. You'd resent that person and want to be rid of him or her as soon as possible.

But what if, in both situations, someone came in and talked to you about your life, identified with your struggles and the difficulties of doing what you do. And then that person explained how he or she was just like you, but had figured a few things out and, with your OK, would like to tell you about the conclusions he or she has come to over time.

You'd probably be more willing to listen—even if you didn't agree with all the conclusions.

Christians may have unintentionally positioned themselves like the intrusive person in the first two scenarios. We try to communicate without credibility. We don't give people the impression that we know how they feel or what their struggles are. We zip straight to the easy answers and expect them to believe us. Why should they? We don't listen to people who aren't credible in our eyes.

As someone who has worked closely with Focus on the Family, I've picked up on one of Dr. James Dobson's biggest secrets of communication. It's something he seems to do instinctively, not as a preplanned technique. Ready? He establishes credibility with his audience before he offers any answers. Read one of his books, watch a video, listen to his radio program. He spends over half of his time connecting with the audience, demonstrating that he knows how they feel. You get the impression that he has crawled into your shoes; he understands your pain and suffering.

And then—only then—will he move on to the answers. I believe it's one of the biggest keys to his popularity, over and above other popular speakers of our time.

What does that have to do with us as writers?

Drama is our chance to establish credibility by *honestly* telling our world that we know how it feels to be lost, lonely, and confused. Even as Christians. If, as we have discussed throughout this book, we bring a deep insight into humanity into our plays, then humanity will be drawn into our plays as well. It's the only way to establish credibility.

And with that credibility comes the chance to offer an answer.

Perspectives and Pet Peeves

Over the years I've compiled a list of one-off thoughts about writing plays, particularly within the Christian market. I keep the list handy because I'm as guilty as the next person of forgetting the truths found there. I pass them on to you for whatever they're worth.

- Private jokes and personal attacks should have no place in your work.

- Don't write about issues, write about *people*. Get to the heart of the matter.

- Don't try to say or do too much in your play. Err to subtlety. Leave people something to think about as they walk away from your play (in other words: let them leave the table hungry).

- Avoid the obvious.

- Don't do anything simply for shock value. Your audience will remember the shock and not the value.

- Be sensible—don't write something that can't be produced in your church or venue (unless you're hired specifically to do it).

- Be open to constructive criticism from those who have read or seen your play. If they didn't understand something, then others probably won't. Maybe it's worth rewriting to clarify.

- Be ready to prove yourself to the leadership in your church or local theatre group. Don't be adversarial in the name of art.

- Be practical. Know your limitations as a writer—not as a means of defeat but as a challenge to eventually overcome them.

ELEVEN

The Last Word

I hope this book has been helpful in your efforts to write plays. Throughout, I've referred to many excellent reference books by writers you should get to know. Read plenty. Soak it all in, then squeeze it back out through your own style and imagination.

I believe—perhaps as much as I believe anything—that the dramatic arts are lost without a meaningful Christian influence. And I believe that our Christian influence is lost without the dramatic arts.

Let's hope and pray that together we can impact our churches, communities, and society with the *honest truth* about following Jesus.

TWELVE

Resources

Here's a concise list of the foremost publishers of religious plays in America (in alphabetical order):

Baker's Plays, 100 Chauncy St., Boston, MA 02111 (617-482-1280)

Contemporary Drama Services, Box 7710, Colorado Springs, CO 80933 (719-594-4422)

Group Books, Box 481, Loveland, CO 80539 (303-669-3836)

Lillenas Drama, 2923 Troost, Kansas City, MO 64109 (816-931-1900)

Word Publishing, 5221 N. O'Connor, Suite 1000, Irving, TX 75039 (1-800-945-3932)

And here's a list of works by the author:

ONE-ACT PLAYS

The Case of the Frozen Saints
A church is dead and Sam Slade is hired to find the killer. Funny—yet pointed in its message about keeping the church alive.

The First Church of Pete's Garage
Dissatisfied with his church, Pete is challenged to start one of his own. Another pointed message administered with lots of comedy.

The Revised Standard Version of Jack Hill
*Based on the musical **A Small Concoction,** this one-act comedy finds Jack Hill mixing a formula in hopes of becoming a more dynamic Christian.*

FULL-LENGTH PLAYS

Fathers Anonymous
A sketch revue exploring the roles fathers play with their spouses, children, and their own fathers.

A Work in Progress

A satirical sketch revue about Christian identity, evangelism, and refrigerator magnets.

Catacombs

A group of Christians hide out in an abandoned mountain church during a time of persecution and discover the meanings of survival, faith, and death.

Family Outings

Realistic comedy and drama exploring the elements that can tear a marriage—and a family—apart.

Pap's Place

A two-act comedy/drama exploring the relationship between three generations of sons—brought together when the grandfather begins to show signs of Alzheimer's disease and a decision must be made about his future.

Snapshots and Portraits

Being single, stubborn fathers and rebellious sons, growing old, single parenting, losing a loved one . . . it's just another day for the Forbes family.

Camp W

Comedy and drama about life for the staffers and campers at the run-down Camp Winikootchi.

Dear Diary

This drama takes us inside the mind of a troubled teenage girl and traces the circumstances in her life that lead her to one conclusion: suicide.

Stop the Presses!

It's 1947 and Ace Tabloid Reporter Jason Bolt is sent on a mission to pose as a would-be assistant pastor to learn the real reason popular evangelist Michael Farley gave up his lucrative ministry to pastor a small mountain church.

MUSICALS

As part of Lillenas' *Season Tickets* Series:

The Faded Flower Christmas Show

A touching one-act play with places for music insertion chronicling the loneliness, heartache, and uplifting faith of a group of elderly people who wait for visitors on Christmas Eve.

A Homemade Christmas
A two-act play with music insertion points about a poor coal-mining family in turn-of-the-century Kentucky who discover the source of Christmas joy during times of hardship.

A Family Christmas
The Graham family is getting ready for Christmas, but somehow the spirit of the season escapes John, the father. In his search to find it, he comes to a surprising conclusion.

Also . . .

A Time for Christmas (music and lyrics by David Clydesdale, Steve Amerson, and Lowell Alexander)
An unpredictable "Ghost of Christmas Past" visits a young man who's too busy for Christmas and takes him on a whirlwind tour of the holiday as it has appeared through the ages.

A Small Concoction (with Tim Albritton)
A "Dr. Jekyll/Mr. Hyde" scenario played out with music and comedy as Jack Hill concocts a formula to become a more dynamic Christian.

The Meaning of Life and Other Vanities (with Tim Albritton)
A musical revue using comedy and drama to uncover the truths of the Book of Ecclesiastes.

Shine the Light of Christmas (music by Dave and Jan Williamson)
A wise aunt explains the importance of a candlelight service by reminiscing about important scenes from her life.

GENERAL RESOURCE

Youth Ministry Comedy and Drama: Better than Bathrobes but Not Quite Broadway (with Chuck Bolte)
A practical guide to drama and comedy in the church. Includes 20 short sketches.

SKETCH COMPILATIONS (AND CHRISTMAS TOO)

Batteries Not Included. *Includes 17 sketches.*

Quick Skits and Discussion Starters (with Chuck Bolte). *Includes 18 sketches and 26 discussion starters.*

Sixty-Second Skits (with Chuck Bolte). *25 thought-provoking sketches dealing with a wide variety of topics.*

Short Skits for Youth Ministry (with Chuck Bolte). *More thought-provoking sketches dealing with a wide variety of topics.*

Sketches of Harvest. *Includes 14 sketches.*

Souvenirs. *Includes 13 sketches.*

Vantage Points. *Includes 17 sketches.*

Void Where Prohibited. *Includes 14 sketches.*

Youth Ministry Comedy and Drama (with Chuck Bolte). *See description above.*

Fast Food. *50 short sketches as discussion starters.*

Drama for Worship, Vol. 1: *On the Street Interview,* plus 11 others.

Drama for Worship, Vol. 2: *The Prodigal and the Pig Farmer,* plus 11 others.

Drama for Worship, Vol. 3: *Complacency,* plus 11 others.

Drama for Worship, Vol. 4: *Conversion,* plus 11 others.

APPENDIX: An Outline

DEATH AT THE BOX OFFICE OUTLINE

by Paul McCusker

(The following outline is © 1990 by Paul McCusker and may not be used without express permission of the author.)

The stage is divided into two halves. Center to stage right is the stage left half of the "inner play" *(Death by Definition)*. It has the look of an Agatha Christie Victorian drawing room. Center to stage left is the off-stage area of the "inner play stage." It is a dump—with ropes and pulleys, fire exit sign, cast-off scenery from long-forgotten productions, a passageway to dressing rooms and stairs for the basement and, shoved into a corner, an industrial metallic desk covered with papers and phone, a time clock hanging next to it, along side a bulletin board on the wall that's covered with recent and age-old notices, clippings, memos, and the like. (In essence, this could be the true backstage of any theatre.)

The Characters:

Dame Gertrude Caldwell (Miss Purple)
Annie Woodenstein, the director of *Death by Definition*
Brett Barrow (Dick Downe)
Desmond Thorne, the theatre manager and resident producer
Peter Codplaice, or better known as "Roach"
Chip Chapman, the playwright
Jonathan Chapman, the playwright's very wealthy father
Katrina Wrenchford, employee of the massive conglomeration that has
    purchased the Box Office as a tax writeoff
Julie Philips (Chartreuse)
Michael Millstone (Jeremy Kennelride-Smith)
Percival, the make-up director for the play
Detective George Fith
Lt. Heather Crescent
John Carey (Dick Downe)
The Big Broadway Producer

ACT ONE
SCENE ONE

We begin with the "drawing room" ending of our play within a play (of course, the audience won't know this). The cast of this play is assembled onstage. Miss Purple—so named because the actress playing her (Dame Gertrude Caldwell) is bordering on senility, barely makes it through her lines, is inclined to launch into a tirade about her glory days at the blink of an eye, and has purple hair—is at the moment of revealing the killer. The moment is climactic. That is, until one character crosses awkwardly in front of another. The director of the play, Annie Woodenstein, shouts from offstage to "hold it" and enters. She is Woody Allen in drag, and we can tell she is at the end of her tether. We also immediately realize that this isn't the actual play, but a rehearsal. Annie "lovingly" (and with great theatrical pretention) chastises the cast, reminding them that the show opens in only a couple of hours. She tells them to take a break, turning to Brett Barrow, the very handsome, very egotistical, compulsive method actor (a cross between Richard Gere in looks and Robert DeNiro in acting intensity), to see if he'll run through the "poison drinking" soliloquy of Dick Downe, one of the inner play's characters.

While they're setting up for that, Desmond Thorne, the British, very caustic and beleaguered producer/theatre manager, enters to find out from Annie how it's going. Following on his heels is a small, dim-witted hedgehog of a man (a miscellaneous do-anything-that-needs-doing sort of person) named Peter Codplaice or, as he is generally known, "Roach." The nickname is no mystery once you get to know him. Roach is carrying a throne and wants to know where to put it on the set. Thorne, with strained patience, explains that he told Roach to get a *phone* for the set. (This is characteristic of Roach and will show up throughout the play.)

In the conversation between Thorne and Annie, then Thorne and Roach, we get a clear picture of what's going on. The Box Office, a tiny off-off-off-off Broadway theatre (Thorne: "We're so far off Broadway, we look for reviews in the Tulsa newspapers"), is in danger of closing due to financial woes. Their potentially final production is a murder-mystery called *Death by Definition* by an obscure, wide-eyed, overenthusiastic would-be playwright named Chip Chapman, who appears during the conversation between Thorne and Annie. Thorne loathes the play and the insipidness of its writer, and he doesn't hide the fact. But we discover, via a threat by Chip, that Thorne had to swallow his loathing because the money for the play was put up by Chip's very rich father, Jonathan Chapman. This production is Thorne's—and the Box Office's—last hope. Which is unfortunate since only a handful of tickets have been sold. "They haven't been *sold*," Thorne reminds us. "They're the comps."

Meanwhile, Brett has been waiting to do his "poison drinking" soliloquy—and does. Within the play, Brett's character is a stereotypical alcoholic has-been financial trader who came to Dunsfold Mansion in hopes of getting his hands on some of the money left in a will by his Uncle Lord Dunsfold. Brett has been left penniless and is now determined to drink himself into an evening of mindless oblivion. (We'll know all this because Brett, eyes closed in concentration to work into an acting frenzy, will ask Annie to "lead him gently to the moment when he picks up the bottle.") Brett performs the soliloquy in a manner that would kill Stanislavski (if he were alive). And we get a glimpse of how awful this play truly is. Nonetheless, Brett pours himself into the part, drinks the alcohol that, in the context of the inner play, is poisoned, sits the glass down, and snaps out of his character. "And I'll die—you don't want me to run that, do you? I want my death to be fresh for the performance tonight." Annie is appreciative but wants him to continue. He snaps back into character and "dies" by collapsing to the floor, writhing and shaking. Annie stops him. "It's too much," she says. Brett argues that writhing and shaking is actually characteristic of death by poison, followed by expulsion of the bowels. Annie hopes he isn't planning on doing such a thing during performance. He thought about it, he confesses. *Don't,* she insists. So, he snaps back into character and reluctantly allows himself to die less dramatically.

Annie is pleased, but instantly interrupted by the arrival of the owner of the Box Office. She's a briefcase-carrying corporate Iron Lady named Katrina Wrenchford, who is only there to represent the mass Conglomeration who bought the Box Office as a tax deferment. She complains about the lack of accommodations for her office. Thorne reminds her that nearly everything but the bare essentials were repossessed—by a finance company owned by the same conglomeration who owns the Box Office, in fact. "We like to keep things in the family," Katrina points out. "We did our best for you," Thorne says. "Sharing an office with the ladies rest room is hardly your best," she replies. "We could switch, if you want," Thorne offers. "I'm in the men's room."

Finally, Annie remembers to tell Brett that the scene's over, he can get up. No response. She approaches him. He won't move. "Not again." She sighs, "These method actors." Katrina doesn't know what to make of this. Annie explains that when Brett gets into a role, he *really* gets into it. At one rehearsal, he stayed dead for a full 45 minutes. They decide to leave him where he is.

Annie calls for the "Mourning Scene" between Miss Purple and "Chartreuse," another character in the inner play who was in love with Brett's character and must react to the news of his death. Another horrible scene; we see how senile Dame Gertrude is as she stumbles through her lines. Chartreuse, on the other hand, is the picture of sweetness and innocence . . . until the scene is ended and we find out that Julie Philips (the actress) is really a jaded, sleazy Hollywood-type who is only doing the play because her last film was a bomb and her agent thought some stage experience would be good for her "image." Chip appears onstage to heap effusive praise on Julie—and we find that he has a massive crush on her. He tells her she *is* Chartreuse, the role was written for her. She tells him to buzz off—she's *not* Chartreuse. It's only a character, after all. (To which we realize that Chip is in love with Julie's stage persona and not who she is in true life.) Then Julie expresses her wish that Brett would snap out of his "death" so they could go get some dinner. (And it may be safe to assume that Julie fancies Brett—which causes Chip to seethe.) At this point, we also meet Michael Millstone, who plays Jeremy Kennel-ride-Smith, the police inspector of our inner play. He is a polite actor, very down-to-earth, who approaches Chip about a particular line in the play he isn't sure about. Still angry from Julie's rebuff, Chip tells him to buzz off.

Percival, the makeup director and rather large, body-building type, enters to announce he wants to schedule makeup for the evening's performance. Annie tells him to start with Brett—who is still on the floor. Katrina enters again to ascertain the meaning of the peculiar Post-it note attached to her Daytimer. It says simply "Death at the Box Office . . . Today!" Thorne enters: "Reviews are in already?"

They discuss the meaning of the note downstage while, unnoticed behind them upstage, Percival is performing CPR and the like on Brett, who remains on the floor, completely unresponsive. (Percival will even send Roach out for an ambulance.) Just as they decide the note may well indeed be a threat—that someone may die—Percival gives up and announces that Brett is *dead!*

Roach arrives with a common household mixer—to which Percival explains that he wanted an *ambulance,* not an *appliance.*

(Blackout)

SCENE TWO

Lights up as the body is being taken out on a stretcher. Thorne is talking with Detective George Fith, who, at a glance, might be confused with the traditional bumbling detective who instead turns out to be clever and shrewd (Columbo, for example). This is not the case. Detective George Fith *is* a bumbling detective. How he rose to the rank of detective is anyone's guess. In the interview as the scene begins, he seems to be asking all the wrong questions and coming to all the wrong conclusions. The detective's assistant, the very attractive Lt. Heather Crescent, guides him along as best as she can without seeming pushy. (She's the one who suspects the wine onstage as being poisoned and sends it off for a toxicological study.) We also learn at this point that word has gotten out about the murder, and the phone has been ringing off the hook for ticket requests. The questions also arise: Why would someone want to kill Brett? who might do it? is it someone in the cast or crew? Det. Fith announces that everyone is under suspicion and not to leave town.

Another question comes up: Will the police close down the theatre? Annie thinks they should take the night off—in honor of the dear, departed Brett. But the powerful Jonathan Chapman (Chip's father) enters in time to intercede. "No!" he says, "as a testimony and memorial to Brett, the show *must* go on!" And Thorne notes: "Besides, the show is sold out." Det. Fith reluctantly agrees, providing there's no foul play. (Which leads to an obvious line from Thorne.)

Randy Winter, a very nervous understudy, is asked to step in for Brett. He's not keen on the idea, for understandable reasons.

Julie is grief-stricken over the loss of Brett—and Chip does everything he can to comfort her. Dame Gertrude steps into the role of Miss Purple and promises to solve this mystery! (And for the rest of this play, she will try—as best as a dithering drool cup of a woman can do such a thing.)

Annie shouts for everyone to get ready for the evening performance—now within an hour from curtain. Thorne, alone on stage with Roach (read: alone), laments about the compromises he's had to make to stay in the world of theatre—and we get an idea of the kinds of absurd productions the Box Office has put on to try to stay afloat (a good opportunity to spoof some of the current trends in theatre). We also find out Roach's motivation for hanging around the Box Office and enduring his caustic employer: he believes he'll get his big chance to become an actor one day soon. "Fat chance," Thorne replies. Roach continues to moan: "But I'll never get a chance to find out if I could be a great actor if they close this theatre down." Thorne observes the irony that if people keep getting murdered, the theatre will make more than enough money to stay open. "Our future is to be determined by a sadistic killer," Thorne says. "Then we should be all right for tonight," Roach responds. Thorne is confused.

"You mean, because of this afternoon." No, *tonight*, Roach reasserts. Thorne doesn't understand. The note about death at the Box Office, Roach says. Thorne agrees—the note said "death at the Box Office—today." Roach corrects him, "Not the note I found taped to the dressing room door a few minutes ago." Roach produces the note and hands it to Thorne. Thorne looks at it, then reads it aloud: "Death at the Box Office—*Tonight!* Roach! Why didn't you show this to someone before?" Roach shrugs, "I didn't think it was important. But now that I know it'll keep me in a job—it's more important than I thought." Thorne groans. "Roach, I want you to go down to the prop room, pick out a sword with a very dull blade—and hack your head off with it." Roach obeys as Annie enters. Thorne, in a moment of weakness, tries to hide the note behind him until, right before Roach leaves, he tells Annie not to ask Thorne about the note. "It puts him in a bad mood," Roach informs her. Annie inquires about the note. Thorne stammers, then finally shows it to her—fully expecting her to want to call the police. She looks at it and talks through the pros and cons of doing anything about it. "If we call the police, they'll close down tonight's show for sure. But if we don't, then someone might get hurt." Much to Thorne's surprise—and ours—Annie decides that the show should go on. "We'll have to be extra careful," she says. "We'll check all the props, make sure there's no poison hanging about, and get through the evening without an incident." Thorne isn't as sure: "You really think we can pull it off?" Annie smiles and crumples up the note: "There will be no death at the Box Office tonight!"

(Blackout)

SCENE THREE

As the lights come up, we see on the inner play stage (stage right) the poison monologue as performed by Randy. He is a nervous wreck about drinking the wine, considering what happened to Brett, and it shows in his performance. Meanwhile, backstage, Thorne and Annie observe anxiously. The scene ends with a blackout (or curtain) on the inner play's stage. Our characters come backstage and we get some chaotic reactions to how the play is going. Randy is still a nervous wreck but is overjoyed that he didn't die. Julie, dressed in a white blouse, is concerned that the audience will die of boredom. Dame Gertrude is oblivious to the world and announces that she thinks she knows who the killer is. For a moment, everyone stops to hear her verdict. She says it's "Jeremy Kennelride-Smith." Everyone relaxes. (That's the killer in the inner play.) Thorne informs her.

Chip comes backstage—all aglow over the premiere of the play. Thorne thinks it's going well (only inasmuch as no one has died). Annie is a nervous wreck and wishes they hadn't gone through with it. "I need a drink," she complains. Thorne says he sent Roach out for some wine.

They hustle and bustle as the next scene begins. It is the scene where Dame Gertrude as Miss Purple informs Chartreuse of Dick Downe's demise. Dame Gertrude butchers her lines. Julie is livid—and it shows in her character. Dame Gertrude exits, saying as she passes Thorne, "I believe it's going quite well, don't you?"

Roach returns with a large ball of twine. "I said *wine*, you imbecile," Thorne says. Annie is beside herself. Thorne rushes to his desk and produces a bottle of something significantly stronger than wine. He pours Annie a glass and gives it to her.

On "stage," Chartreuse turns to someone out of our line of vision (since we're only seeing half of the inner play stage) and speaks vindictively. A shot rings out, Chartreuse clutches her stomach, and blood soaks through the white blouse. Annie and Thorne react backstage—there wasn't supposed to be any blood after the shot. Michael Millstone as Jeremy Kennelride-Smith rushes to Chartreuse and continues with the lines from the play, not realizing that something is amiss. As he proclaims his secret love for her (part of the inner play), his hand touches her bloody hand. Out of character, he is startled, then realizes the blood is soaking through the shirt. Entirely out of character, he cries out, "Good Lord! Kill the lights! She's been shot! *Really* shot!"

Blackout on stage right as Thorne, Millstone, and Randy carry Julie offstage and lay her down. It is utter confusion as they all talk over each other. Annie says, "I should have known it would happen! It's all my fault!" Thorne shouts for someone to call an ambulance ("Not *you*, Roach!"). Millstone is stricken, someone must've put real bullets in the gun! Someone observes that the show is getting a standing ovation by the audience.

Meanwhile, Julie is attempting to move. They insist she lay still until the ambulance arrives. Chip breaks through to say a few last words to his beloved. His speech is eloquent. In the somber silence, she tells him to buzz off, then insists that they shut up and get away from her. She wasn't shot, she tells them. She used a blood-bag to pump some life into her death. This is followed by unanimous relief. Thorne and Annie embrace. "The note was wrong! No one will die at the Box Office tonight!" At which point the entire cast and crew turn on them for taking such a risk. Thorne insists it worked out for the best. "Explain it to them, Annie," he says. Annie steps forward to do that but, before she can say very much, she begins choking and gagging. She clutches her throat and collapses on the floor. Thorne examines her and declares that she is, indeed, dead at the Box Office!

(Blackout. End of Act One.)

ACT TWO
SCENE ONE

It is a week later. No one has died in a while and the fortunes of the Box Office are shifting. Where *Death by Definition* initially had full houses and received rave reviews—much to Thorne's chagrin—it more recently began to receive bad editorials that deplored a play that seemed to exploit the darker side of human nature, chastising playgoers for wanting to see someone die onstage. And, frankly, people began to recognize it for what it really was: a bad play.

Additionally, we see Thorne having to deal with would-be suicides who are desperate to audition for the show.

The police still haven't caught the killer and have run out of clues. (Thorne: What do all the victims have in common? / Roach: They're all dead!) Thorne informs us, through Roach, that he's been conducting a little investigation of his own.

Katrina Wrenchford is putting pressure on Thorne again. She wants the Box Office to remain profitable. Now that the Conglomeration Conglomerate has gotten a taste of the money in theatre, they want more. Here, as before, we get the sense that Thorne and Wrenchford have a deep-rooted dislike for one another.

And we also learn that a big Broadway producer is coming in secret to see the show, likely that night. Thorne isn't happy because the audiences are dwindling. He almost wishes that someone would die, or they'll lose their big chance.

Thorne concocts a scheme. Get one of the "would-be" suicides to fake a death and skip town. Thorne believes this will pack the house again in time for the Broadway producer's visit. He selects John Carey, a Vietnam vet who lost more than the war there.

Just before the matinee, another mysterious note shows up saying "Death at the Box Office at Two." And, sure enough, John Carey dies while putting on his makeup (poison absorbed through the skin).

Word gets out, and ticket sales increase for that evening's performance. Thorne is pleased but concerned that someone else has died.

Unexpectedly, Det. Fith and Lt. Crescent show up and now, on the verge of a big Broadway production deal, they threaten to close everything down. Thorne announces he's come up with another brilliant plan, but it requires using someone as bait. All eyes turn to Roach.

(Blackout)

SCENE TWO

We begin the scene with a scene from *Death by Definition*. This time, instead of a handsome leading man, we see Roach as Dick Downe— botching the lines and making a general mess of things. He interacts with the other characters in the scene preceding the "poison" soliloquy, they leave as written, then he butchers the soliloquy itself. He picks up the drink. Offstage, Det. Fith and Lt. Crescent are alarmed. Thorne assures them that it's empty. Roach drinks, then spits out a mouthful of liquid. He turns to Thorne and says, "I thought you said this was empty!" and collapses onto the floor. Det. Fith dashes onto the stage—reacts to the audience shyly, then in an amateurish hamlike manner—goes to Roach and announces what we already assume. Roach is dead. This gets a standing ovation from the audience.

SCENE THREE

Later. Lights come up in time to see Roach's sheet-covered form being carried off. The cast is assembled on both the "stage" and off-stage. Det. Fith wants to ask everyone some questions now that the audience is gone. He uses every ounce of skill he has, which isn't much, to ask all the wrong questions and get everyone confused. Dame Gertrude announces that *she* knows who the murderer is, but everyone tells her to sit down and shut up. Lt. Crescent steps forward to offer her perspective—which is far more intelligent than her boss's. She maintains that the murders were definitely committed by someone in the cast or crew who had a vested interest in the success of the play.

But *who* stands to gain the most?

Suddenly, Chip stands up and shouts defensively, "I know what you're thinking! You're thinking it's me! But I've been doing some investigating of my own, and I can tell you who the murderer *really* is!"

(Blackout)

Thorne steps forward, speaking in the darkness. "Er, excuse me. He said he knows who the murderer is, not "turn off the lights like it's the end of the scene."

The lights come up again.

Thorne: Thank you. Now, Chippy. Who is the murderer?

Chip: We all are!—when we take a play like mine and kill it with poor acting, when we kill our audiences with mediocrity, and on and on with an idealistic rally speech about integrity in the arts.

They endure this to the end whereupon Thorne tells him to get stuffed and announces that *he* knows who the murderer is!

(Blackout)

In the darkness, Thorne speaks again. "Er, excuse me, but . . . could I have the lights back on, please?"

Lights up.

Thorne: Thanks. (You really need to get your cues straight.)

Thorne now reveals all that he has discovered in his own little investigation. Miss Purple is really a man. Michael Millstone is really a woman. Percival is really an ex-wrestler for Saturday morning television. Det. Fith is really an idiot. And Julie Philips is really a model built from a kit by a plastic surgeon. Katrina Wrenchford is really Jonathan Chapman. (Not really, but he says so.) And the murderer?

Thorne says simply: The murderer is . . . *me.*

Gasp.

Thorne then brags egotistically about his ingenius plot, how he did it, and all the acclaim he'll get in the world of theatre. He's even writing a play about the whole scheme, which he expects will bring him a comfortable living once he's paroled on good behavior.

Unable to stand it anymore, Chip Chapman suddenly pulls a gun and tells Thorne to shut up. He then confesses that *he's* the killer and the glory is all *his.* And now we see a Chip we haven't seen before: no longer is he a wispy, naive, would-be playwright, but a cold, calculating and confident murderer. Julie Philips is turned on by the thought. Chip announces he'll now make good his escape, but insists on taking a hostage. Julie volunteers. Chip accepts. Thorne laughs and assures him he won't escape—the gun is a prop and Roach, who isn't dead after all, has gone for the police. Whereupon Roach arrives with a *priest,* having messed up the request again. Fortunately, the priest knows karate and knocks Chip out when he tries to leave.

Det. Fith and Lt. Crescent take control of the situation, and we now discover how Thorne drew the killer out. He explains that the ego angle is a sure-bet among theatre people because they always want the credit for their work. He knew if he tried to take the credit for the murders, the real murderer would've gone crazy.

Everyone but Thorne and Roach exit. Thorne is contented that the case is solved. Roach asks why there was liquid in the wine bottle when it was supposed to be empty. Thorne shrugs, he thought it was empty too. "But . . . I could be dead!" Roach complains. "Hope springs eternal," Thorne says. Thorne sniffs the bottle, withdrawing suddenly. "From the smell of this stuff, you *should* be dead. I think this might be real poison. Better get rid of it." Thorne is about to do this when Katrina comes on with the Big Broadway producer. He wants the show on Broadway, says he'll meet with them the next day, and exits. After he goes, Katrina states that she has fired Thorne and will coproduce the show herself on behalf of the Conglomeration. She ridicules him for botching up the entire week's performances and destroying the fine reputation of the Box Office theatre. "So, you're fired, Thorne. Do you understand?"

Thorne seems to take this gracefully. "That's all right," he says. "I'll find work elsewhere in this town."

"Over my dead body," Katrina says, smiling viciously. "No hard feelings, though. This is strictly business."

Thorne smiles as he pours her a drink. "Let's drink to that." He hands her the glass. "To our respective futures!"

She salutes and drinks while Thorne watches her.

"To Death at the Box Office." He smiles and salutes in return.

(Blackout. End of the play.)

Endnotes

1. Rob Rucker, *Producing and Directing Drama for the Church* (Kansas City: Lillenas Publishing Co., 1993), 21.

2. C. S. Lewis, *English Literature in the Sixteenth Century,* Book Three: *Verse in the "Golden" Period* (Oxford: Oxford University Press, 1954), 529.

3. Nigel Forde, *Theatrecraft: An Actor's Notes on His Trade* (London: MARC Europe, 1986), 6.

4. Ibid., 6-7.

5. Murray Watts, *Christianity and the Theatre* (Edinburgh: Handsel Press, 1986), 27.

6. J. B. Phillips, *The Ring of Truth* (Wheaton, Ill.: Harold Shaw Publishing Co., 1967), 21.

7. Louis Catron, *The Elements of Playwriting* (New York: Macmillan Publishing Co., 1993), 4.

8. Nigel Forde, "All Play and No Work . . . ," *Riding Lights Theatre Company Newsletter,* 1993.

9. Theodore Baehr, *Getting the Word Out* (San Francisco: HarperCollins Publishers Inc., 1986), xv.

10. W. H. Auden, as quoted in Forde, *Theatrecraft,* title page.

11. Forde, *Theatrecraft,* 15.

12. Catron, *Elements of Playwriting,* 19.

13. Ibid., 28.

14. Bernard Grebanier, *Playwriting: How to Write for the Theater* (New York: Harper-Collins Publishers Inc., 1961), 23.

15. Forde, *Theatrecraft,* 95.

16. Lajos Egri, *The Art of Dramatic Writing,* (New York: Simon and Schuster, 1960), 100.

17. John Gardner, *The Art of Writing Fiction* (New York: Alfred A. Knopf, Inc., 1983), 201.

18. Gardner, *Art of Writing Fiction,* 10.